ANTIQUE FINISHING FOR BEGINNERS

Other Books by Frederic Taubes

Abracadabra and Modern Art
Acrylic Painting for the Beginner
Anatomy of Genius
Better Frames for Your Pictures
Modern Art Sweet and Sour
New Essays on Art
New Techniques in Painting
Oil Painting and Tempera
Painting Techniques, Ancient and Modern
Pen and Ink Drawing
Pictorial Anatomy of the Human Body
Pictorial Composition and the Art of Drawing
Restoring and Preserving Antiques
Studio Secrets
Taubes' Paintings and Essays on Art
The Amateur Painter's Handbook
The Art and Technique of Landscape Painting
The Mastery of Oil Painting
The Painter's Dictionary of Materials and Methods
The Painter's Question and Answer Book
The Quickest Way to Draw Well
The Quickest Way to Paint Well
The Technique of Oil Painting
The Technique of Portrait Painting
The Technique of Still Life Painting
You Don't Know What You Like

ANTIQUE FINISHING FOR BEGINNERS

BY FREDERIC TAUBES

WATSON-GUPTILL PUBLICATIONS, New York

First published 1972 in New York by Watson-Guptill Publications,
a division of Billboard Publications, Inc.,
165 West 46 Street, New York, N.Y.

Manufactured in Hong Kong

First Printing, 1972

Library of Congress Cataloging in Publication Data

Taubes, Frederic, 1900–
   Antique finishing for beginners.

   1. Wood finishing. 2. Metals—Finishing. I. Title.
TT325.T38   684'.084   76–190523
ISBN 0-8230-0230-6

Foreword

This book is designed for the novice who has not developed his manual skills sufficiently to employ the more elaborate processes described in my earlier book, *Restoring and Preserving Antiques,* which is geared to both professionals and nonprofessionals. With few exceptions, the processes described in *Restoring and Preserving Antiques* dealt with objects of value —the restoration and preservation of genuine antiques of all periods, ranging from utilitarian objects to works of fine art. By restoration I always mean elimination, or rather amelioration, of disfigurements that may have deprived the object of its esthetic appeal. Under no circumstances in my former book do I suggest tampering with the object's ancient patina —unless it has become lost due to some accident or an imprudent earlier restoration; in that case re-establishment of the ancient patina would be mandatory.

In this book I will focus on objects that possess no value as antiques, or perhaps no value at all. My aim will be to make these objects both useful and beautiful. Of course, the designation "beautiful" may be subject to all kinds of interpretations, some of them quite contradictory. To avoid the pitfalls encountered when dealing with objects of fashionable appeal (always transitory in nature), I shall concentrate on producing those effects that distinguish *bona fide* antiques—effects that are broadly connected with the condition of "patina."

Introduction

Ancient patina! It ennobles objects; it endows them with a surface quality totally absent in things newly fashioned. Ancient patina is a quality that characterizes antiques of all descriptions; it is a precious quality—provided that there is an inherent beauty in the ancient object. However, this antique patina—and an antique appearance in general—can be conjured up at will by the judicious hand of the craftsman who has not only the technical know-how but good taste as well.

How do you acquire good taste? In this regard, I have no ready-made formula. All I can say is that by close study and observation in the leading antique shops and in the museums you may acquire an understanding of what makes objects beautiful. In mentioning the museums, I have in mind those that display works of art and decoration, as well as utilitarian objects of the past ages—specifically the pre-machine ages, not later than the first quarter of the nineteenth century. Whatever has happened in the field of decoration (not fine arts) after that date is of dubious, not to say outright poor, taste. Unless an object produced after that date derives its configurations from an ancient pattern—or relies on technological simplicity—you may find that I am right.

I mentioned *good taste* and *technical know-how*. Technical know-how is important, but not necessarily identical with professional skill. Professional skill can only be attained by applying yourself seriously to the task at hand—learning the ropes, as it were. However, a modicum of know-how can help the novice achieve good results, even if he possesses only modest manual skills. I shall direct my instructions to the novice. If carefully followed, these instructions should produce gratifying results.

Contents

ANTIQUE FINISHING FOR BEGINNERS

1

Materials and Their Uses

A great variety of different materials could be employed to achieve effects that are identical, or nearly identical, to those described in this book, but my aim was to simplify all procedures and to limit the equipment to an absolute minimum. Therefore, I have chosen materials that are readily available and applicable to the diverse tasks described in this book. With few exceptions, I obtained all of them in hardware, paint, artists' supply, and drug stores, and their cost is low. In no case, however, did I sacrifice quality for price.

Materials for Conditioning Wood

These are the materials that you will use for basic operations on raw, untreated wood.

Sandpaper. This is a general term for abrasive papers of all kinds. You use it to smooth out the rough surface of wood. You will be using the type of abrasive paper called carborundum. You will need four grades: medium, coarse, medium fine, fine, and polishing paper. A wooden holder keeps the sandpaper in place while you are rubbing and saves your hands (Figure 1).

Wood sealers. These are available under various brand names. However, we will use the acrylic medium for sealing wood. On small surfaces you may use a clear plastic spray such as Blair produced by Behlen Bro., or you can try one called Krylon. You can also use this spray to give an object a high gloss.

Wood stains. Concentrated tea provides a light yellowish stain while coffee, used in various concentrations, yields a brown stain. You can pro-

Figure 1. This wooden sandpaper holder keeps the piece of sandpaper in place and provides a sturdy grip for your hand.

duce similar effects with a greatly diluted umber acrylic paint. Yellow oxide and raw and burnt siena acrylic colors, when sufficiently diluted with water or acrylic medium, are also useful for staining. A warm, orangy color can be obtained from orange shellac, but it will also make the wood's surface glossy. The aniline dyes, known in the trade as penetrating oil stains, have become rather obsolete. We will use only the mahogany stain, because there is no acrylic color that can substitute for it.

Wood bleaches. Clorox, the common laundry bleach, can be used on wood, but its action is quite slow. A much more powerful bleach is produced by Behlen Bro.; it is really two preparations—a color dissolvent and a decolorant—which you use consecutively. There are other efficient bleaching agents on the market as well.

Paint removers. Removers, such as those sold under the brand name Red Devil, dissolve old varnish, lacquers, oil paints, and acrylic paints. There are other brands that may be equally effective.

Materials to achieve a high gloss. There are several materials which will give the surface of raw wood a high gloss: acrylic medium, clear plastic spray (Behlen, Krylon, and Blair are brands that I recommend), and commercial wax in liquid and paste form.

Materials for Repairing Wood Surfaces

Often you will need to fill in cracks and holes or make minor missing parts. There are various crack fillers which are miscible with water, such as Durham Rockhard Water Putty or Duralite Wood Dough, but in this book I use acrylic modeling paste. Like the other wood fillers, its white color can be altered to match the color of the wood surface by mixing it with any appropriate acrylic color.

Materials for Patinas on Wood

Patina is a term that refers to the change that takes place in the surface of an object, usually made of metal or polychromed wood, over a period of years. When refinishing ordinary objects to look like antiques (or restoring *bona fide* antiques), your objective is to simulate or restore this patina which adds so much to the beauty of objects.

White gesso and raw or burnt umber. These two acrylic colors mixed together produce a gray paint which is the foundation of all patina work done to wood. As the gray paint is rubbed into the surface of the wood, it becomes imbedded into its minute openings. Here, and also in such places as the joints in a molding, it will accumulate much as dust does in a *bona fide* antique. In real antiques, such an accumulation of dust is often found in a petrified state.

Design Materials

Several parts of this book are devoted to creating designs on the surface of various objects. Here is a list of materials that you will need.

Brushes. You need only four different brushes for all the designs and procedures described: a utility brush 1½″ wide, a flat soft-hair brush 1″ wide, and two round sable or sabeline brushes, numbers 1 and 4. The sable are more expensive than the sabeline (Figure 2) but more useful for precise work.

Compasses. For producing circular designs, you'll need two compasses: one small and one much larger (Figure 3).

Markers. You'll need a thin-tipped nylon marker (Figure 3) and one with a large felt tip. These should contain a black aniline dye, not a water-soluble dye (Figure 4).

Masking tape. This is a pressure-sensitive paper tape. You use it to mask along the straight lines of parts of designs that should be protected from paint.

Maskoid. This is a quick-drying liquid similar to rubber cement. It is applied with a brush; when it has dried, you can peel it off. You use it to isolate ornaments or parts of the design that should be kept free from paint.

Ruler. You'll need a wooden ruler 24″ or longer for drawing rectangular patterns. To prevent the ruler from slipping, glue strips of sandpaper to its reverse side.

T-Square. This is used for drawing perpendicular and horizontal straight lines (Figure 5).

Triangle. Choose one made of transparent plastic (Figure 5).

X-Acto knife. This is used to cut templets—paper or metal patterns for

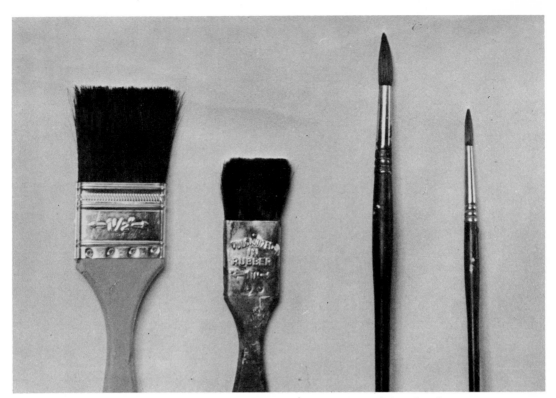

Figure 2. From left to right the brushes are: a utility brush, a flat, soft-hair brush, and two round sable brushes.

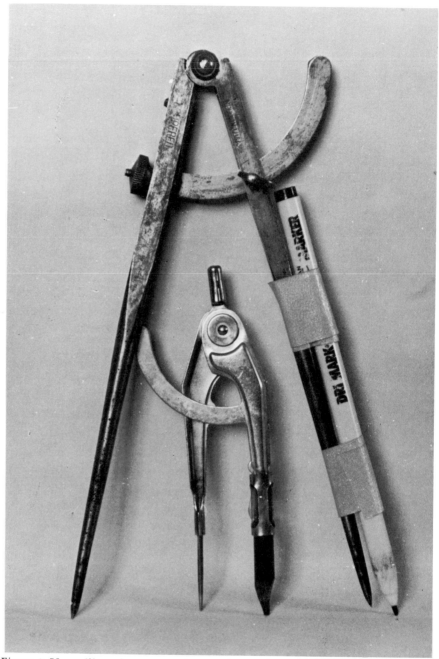

Figure 3. You will need compasses in two sizes: a large one and a small one. The large compass has a nylon-tipped marker attached to it.

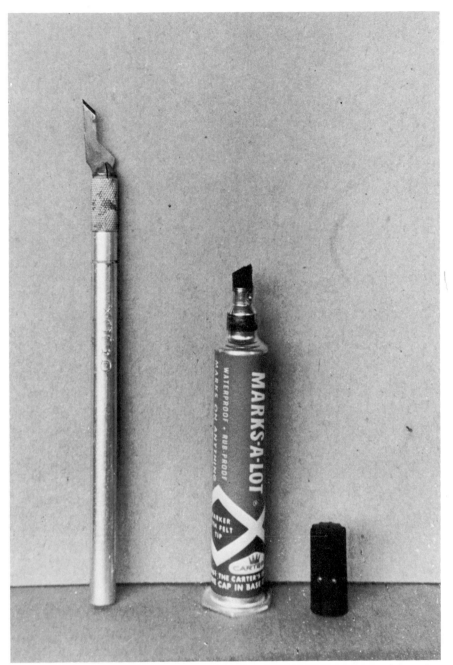

Figure 4. This felt-tipped marker, like the nylon-tipped one, is useful in delineating designs on the objects you may want to finish. On its left, you can see an X-Acto knife with a blade used for cutting straight lines.

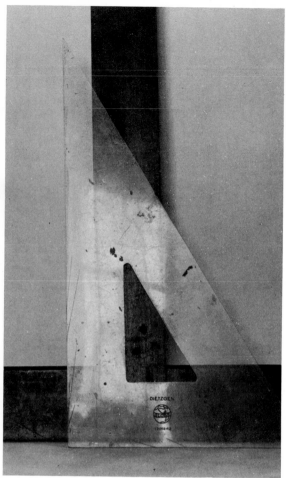

Figure 5. Pictured here are a wooden T-square and a plastic triangle. Both are useful in creating straight lines in your designs.

Figure 6. An X-Acto knife has interchangeable blades: one type is used for cutting along straight lines (seen in Figure 4); the other used for cutting curves is seen here.

designs. You need two blades: one for cutting along straight lines, the other for cutting along curved lines (Figure 6).

Texturing and patterning materials. When these are applied to or drawn across wet acrylic paint, they produce textures and patterns. You'll need cheesecloth, soft paper, sponges of various textures, and rubber combs (Figure 7).

Coloring Materials

There are two basic coloring materials, acrylic paints and spray enamel paints. Acrylic paints are used with acrylic medium or water while spray enamels are used directly from their aerosol cans.

Acrylic paints. These are water-based, synthetic resin colors. They dry quickly; once they are dry, they become insoluble in water. However, you can easily remove them with lacquer solvent or a paint remover. When used undiluted, one or two applications of an acrylic will cover any underlying color. You can also dilute acrylic paints to any degree with water or the acrylic medium Diluted, these colors serve as excellent wood stains. Not only wood but any conceivable (hard) surface, even glass, can be painted with this material. However, glass objects thus treated are not washable, because moisture penetrating through minute openings in the paint film strips the paint off the surface.

Acrylic colors are obtainable in tubes, where their consistency is firmer, or in jars, where it is more liquid. Commercial acrylic house paints, sold in pint and larger cans, do well only for use as base colors when you are treating larger objects.

The designation of the acrylic colors is not uniform with the various manufacturers. The names of the colors of these paints do not always conform with the nomenclature common to artist's colors. Here is a basic list of colors: white (to save money, buy cans of white acrylic gesso instead of tube white), black, raw umber, burnt umber, raw siena, burnt siena, red oxide, yellow, ochre, phthalocyanine blue (hereafter called phthalo blue), and phthalocyanine green (hereafter called phthalo green). You can add other colors to the list.

Acrylic medium. A milky liquid of low viscosity, it serves as thinner for acrylic colors; it produces a glossy finish. For a mat finish, water should be used as a thinner. Acrylic medium also serves as a sealer for wood and as a "varnish" to produce a glossy surface.

Figure 7. Three rubber combs with various sized teeth are embedded in a triangular piece of wood. Each comb produces a distinctive pattern.

Attention: I have been referring on many occasions to the acrylic products. Since I am only familiar with those acrylic products bearing the brand name Liquitex, produced by Permanent Pigments, Cincinnati, Ohio, you may not achieve results similar to mine if you employ a different brand.

Spray enamels. These are sold in aerosol cans in a great variety of colors (including metallic colors of gold, silver, and copper) under the trade names: Jet Spray Alkyd Enamels (H. Behlen & Bro.), Krylon, Blair, etc. Besides the clear plastic spray, your list should include the following nonmetallic colors: yellow, black, white, and red; any other color can be added if desired. Like all spray paints, they are easy to apply and provide an extremely even and glossy finish on nonabsorbent surfaces. It should be mentioned that the designation of colors differs among various manufacturers; therefore no specific names of colors have been mentioned.

Gilding Materials

Gilding with leaves, fully described in my earlier book, *Restoring and Preserving Antiques,* is not a very difficult task, but it requires a certain skill that a beginner might not possess. Therefore, we will be using *wax gilt* (obtainable in art supply stores) sold under the trade name *Treasure Gold Wax Gilt.* This is the trade name of a wax gilt produced by the Connoisseur Studio (P.O. Box 7887, Louisville, Kentucky 40207). The formula was originally established by the author and published in *Studio Secrets* (Watson-Guptill, 1943). Wax gilt represents the easiest form of gilding and applying other metallic coatings such as that of silver, brass, pewter, copper, and a few other "exotic" tints. We will require one of the following waxes: "fire gold" (this is the brightest color), "brass" (for an all-purpose gold effect), and "Renaissance gold" (a deep, antique red-gold).

Silver and pewter wax. These are also useful products. The pewter wax closely approximates old, darkened silverleaf applications.

Metallic spray enamels. These come in aerosol cans under various trade names such as Jet Spray (Behlen Bro.), Krylon, Blair, etc. The most useful metallic colors are gold, copper, and silver or aluminum.

Agate burnisher. This tool is used to burnish wax gilt, gold paint, and acrylic surfaces to a high gloss. A steel burnisher, such as the one used

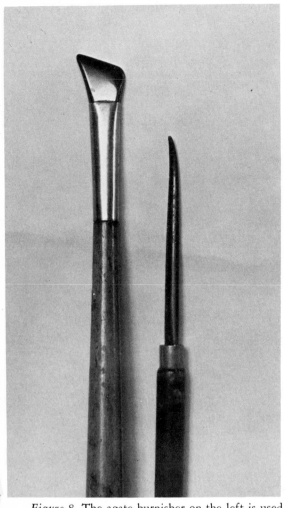

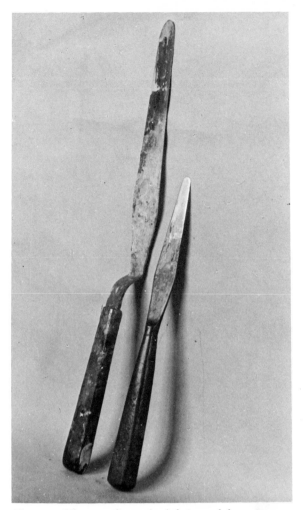

Figure 8. The agate burnisher on the left is used to polish wax gilt to a high gloss. The steel burnisher on the right is a fair substitute and is much less expensive.

Figure 9. The spatula on the left is used for mixing paint and the palette knife on the right is used for filling in cracks with modeling paste.

on copper plates in etching, is a fair substitute for the former, but its action is not as perfect as that of the more expensive burnisher made of agate (Figure 8).

Orange shellac. This is used for the protection and the antiquing of gilded surfaces.

Burnt umber. This acrylic color can be used to produce patinas on gildings.

Materials for Patinas on Metals

A complete list of the various processes for creating patinas on metal is contained in *Restoring and Preserving Antiques.* The following list of chemicals and polishes will be sufficient for the operations described in this book.

Liver of sulphuric (potassium polysulfide). It comes in yellowish, amorphous lumps and dissolves easily in warm water. In a solution of 1:6 (the first by weight, the second by volume), it will oxidize silver to a darker or even black color, depending on how long the silver is exposed to it. It can be used to make recessive surfaces contrast with the high gloss of raised parts.

Silver polish. Any commercial product will serve the purpose well.

Salt and vinegar. In a saturated solution, these ingredients can produce a greenish-blue patination on copper, bronze, and brass.

Iron chloride. A noncorrosive acid salt (that is, nonharmful to your skin and breathing), it is used for etching copper plates. It comes in solid irregular lumps and dissolves readily in water. In a concentration of 1:4 (the first by weight, the second by volume) it will provide a brownish-green, antique patina on objects made of copper and its alloys.

Sulphuric acid. Used in the concentration found in automobile batteries, it will "antique" modern pewter. In a weaker concentration, it will clean badly oxidized silver and copper.

Adhesives

The following list of adhesives will be useful in various operations described later.

White synthetic glue. This is sold under various trade names such as Elmer's. It generally comes in a plastic squeeze bottle. It provides a strong bond and is useful in many processes such as adhering a linen covering to a wooden insert.

Quick Stick adhesive. This is a type of rubber cement in an aerosol can, particularly suitable for the attachment of paper templets.

Rubber cement. This is also used for attaching paper templets.

Acrylic medium and acrylic modeling paste. These also possess adhesive properties. However, these materials are not strong enough to be used for joining wood.

Miscellaneous Materials and Tools

The following items are indispensable in refinishing antiques:

Palette knife. This instrument will be used in connection with repairs of objects made of stone. We will also use it for filling in cracks, holes, and undesirable irregularities in wood. It should have a blade of about 4″ long, neither too stiff nor too elastic (Figure 9).

Spatula. This trowel-shaped knife (Figure 9) is useful for mixing paint and scraping off paint that has been softened with paint remover.

Wax. Two kinds of waxes should be considered; one in paste form, another in liquid form. The popular, commercial brands are of such high quality that the naming of a particular one would be pointless.

2

Finishing Wood Surfaces

Before doing any work on a wood surface, its texture must be considered. Is it rough or smooth? If the wood surface is rough, sandpapering is indicated.

Sandpapering

Begin your sandpapering with a medium coarse carborundum paper; then use a medium fine paper. If you want a perfectly smooth surface, finish the sanding with a polishing paper.

Always sandpaper with, never against, the grain. When sandpapering straight surfaces, the use of a sandpaper holder (Figure 1) facilitates the work considerably. When it is necessary to sand moldings or other rounded surfaces, wrap your abrasive paper around dowel sticks of appropriate thicknesses. When you complete your sanding, remove all the accumulated sawdust from the wood's surface.

Filling in Minor Cracks and Holes

We will be using acrylic modeling paste for our repairing. You can use the paste either in its original white color, or you can match it to the color of the surface you are repairing by mixing an appropriate acrylic color with it.

You can also match the color of the paste after you apply it to the crack. However, its consistency should be thicker. You can accomplish this by placing the paste on an absorbent paper, such as newsprint, or by exposing it to air. This allows some of the paste's binder (the acrylic medium) to evaporate.

Step-by-Step Filling Procedure

You should be able to repair most minor cracks with the brief procedure that follows:

Step 1. Take a little acrylic modeling paste on a palette knife and press the paste into the crack (Figure 10).

Step 2. If the hole is deep, you will need several successive applications. Always allow the preceding application to dry before starting the subsequent one.

Step 3. When the paste is dry, sandpaper the surface to smooth out any protrusions left by the paste. By slightly wetting the dry surface, you can facilitate the sanding.

Filling Deep Cracks

For cracks deeper than ¼", the paste should be mixed with fine sawdust to create a rather dense putty—one that you can knead like dough. To increase the attachment of this putty, brush some of the acrylic medium into the gap to be filled.

Thick applications of paste that *do not* contain sawdust will develop fissures upon drying. But these do not weaken the body of the material; they can be covered by a subsequent application. Note that if you do not mix the paste with sawdust, you should use layers of limited thickness (about ⅛") at one time. Then, permit each layer to dry before further buildup of the material. Thin layers will dry rapidly; the thicker the application, the slower the drying of the entire mass. Of course, heat can be used to accelerate drying.

Once dry, you can drill, file, or cut the modeling paste with a saw or knife. Sandpapering of the perfectly dry paste is not easy. Hence, it is advisable to sand down the paste with abrasive paper before it hardens completely, that is, as soon as the paste loses its semisoft consistency. To avoid awkward ridges that may remain and to bring the filled-in spot flush with the surface of the wood, meticulous sandpapering of the adjoining areas is needed.

Figure 10. Minor cracks and holes in wooden surfaces can be repaired with acrylic modeling paste. A palette knife provides a handy applicator for the paste.

Flat Finishes on Softwoods

I'll be referring to certain categories of wood. I suggest that these be given particular tints which I call "natural." By this I mean that these tints will not cover up the grain of the wood, but provide a transparent finish, or stain. Take, for example, knotty pine paneling. When properly stained, the richness of the wood's grain is markedly enhanced, because its soft and hard parts, as well as the knots, take on different colors. Other softwoods that can be stained in the same fashion are basswood and aspen, but their grain lacks the interest of knotty pine.

Freshly cut softwoods—pine, spruce, and most of the semisoft varieties —are light in color; they must be tinted in a certain manner. When exposed to light, air, and especially to outdoor conditions, all lumber will darken to various degrees, even to the point of becoming almost black. Wood improperly stained, whether in a natural or artificial manner, will have to be bleached using the products mentioned in Chapter 1.

Staining with Tea and Coffee

As mentioned in Chapter 1, concentrated tea rubbed on a raw wood surface will produce a light yellowish stain. Coffee when applied to raw wood yields a brown stain (see page 49). When treating a wood surface in such a way, proceed as follows: first dip a sponge into the solution of coffee or tea. Work the saturated sponge vigorously into the grain of the wood (Figure 11). For darker effects, repeat this procedure after allowing every application to dry well.

Staining with Acrylic Colors

A wider range of stains can be obtained with acrylic paints. If a bright, yellowish color appears to be indicated, yellow oxide will be appropriate; a dull, yellowish-brown color can be produced with raw umber. Burnt umber—unless well thinned with water—will darken wood to a deep brown which, unless covered with a patina, is rarely desirable. I shall discuss this process of *antiquing* or *patining* later in this chapter.

Producing a Red Stain

Burnt siena acrylic paint produces a reddish color. If used on pine or spruce, its reddish color would falsify their character. But burnt siena is

Figure 11. Coffee or tea stains and thinned acrylic paints can be applied to large wooden surfaces with a sponge.

quite useful for certain types of wood, such as cherry or gum wood. As for creating a deep red mahogany color, it can not be done with acrylics; as mentioned in Chapter 1, only a penetrating oil stain will provide such an effect.

Flat Finishes on Hardwoods

As a rule, flat finishes on cherry, walnut, and related hardwoods do not enhance their beauty. Such woods (as well as mahogany) should show a high degree of polish. Maple, birch, oak, and chestnut can be treated with light stains. When richly grained and left with a flat finish oak and chestnut show a very attractive texture.

Most of the hardwoods cannot be stained easily with tea or coffee solutions; acrylic colors are much more appropriate for staining them. To apply these colors, use a piece of rag instead of a sponge or brush. Saturate the rag with the acrylic and vigorously work it into the grain of the wood.

Cherry can be stained lightly with burnt siena, but burnt siena would not work well on walnut. Waxing (or varnishing) alone will deepen the natural color of walnut and that is all that should be done to it.

The reddish deep, dark color of mahogany was often used in nineteenth-century furniture. When mahogany appears in solid boards (not veneers), bleaching it to a honey-colored tone will change its character and quite often enhance its appearance. When I mention veneer, I have in mind furniture in the Empire and Regency style and the late Victorian period.

Glossy Finishes on Softwoods

There are no hard and fast rules as to when a wood surface should be flat or when it should be glossy. As a general rule, glossy surfaces if quite large—take, for example, a paneling of very dark knotty pine—are not attractive. However, a table top made of the same wood can not be glossy enough; here a mirror-like finish is always desirable. Thus, when dealing with objects made of wood—hard or soft—their particular nature will suggest the most appropriate treatment.

After rendering your wood surface both smooth by sandpapering and nonabsorbent by means of the acrylic medium, use any good commercial wax on it and polish it to a high gloss. After an initial treatment with the acrylic medium, small objects can be sprayed with clear pastic spray.

A glossy surface can also be achieved by shellacking. If you use orange shellac, a very pleasant, bright orangy tone will result. If your wood's surface has been previously stained to a darker color, the application of orange shellac will produce an "antique" finish, such as that seen on early American pine furniture.

Glossy Finishes on Hardwoods

Certain hardwoods such as walnut, cherry, and maple do not show the design of their grain to their best advantage unless they are polished to a high gloss. The same applies to practically all the exotic, richly-grained woods and also to mahogany of a uniform dark color. However, this type of mahogany, if previously stained, looks particularly attractive when bleached to a honey-colored lightness.

When sufficiently smooth and nonporous, hardwoods will attain a gloss when merely waxed. When sprayed with clear plastic spray such wood does not require sealing. The spray, more than any other coating, will create a maximum gloss. However, it is always advisable to employ wax as the final finish of a glossy surface.

As mentioned, the smoothness of the surface of wood and its absorbency will aid in achieving a high gloss. Hardwood is less absorbent than softwood; some types of hardwood, such as oak, will attain a high polish when merely waxed. As a rule, one application of the acrylic medium rubbed into the surface of a hardwood with a cheesecloth, plus subsequent waxing, will create a glossy surface.

Patinas on Raw Wood

In order to simulate or reproduce the patina, that is, the surface quality and color of an old object, use your acrylic colors. Begin with acrylic gesso which is white in color and identical with the white acrylic sold in jars and tubes; however acrylic gesso has a more liquid consistency. This acrylic gesso when mixed with raw or burnt umber acrylic paint produces a thin gray solution. When it drys, this mixture of white acrylic gesso and umber acrylic simulates the patina found on old wooden objects which is actually "petrified dust"—one of the touchstones of their antiquity.

Whether produced on soft or hardwoods, the process of creating patinas will be identical. However, not all kinds of wood are equally

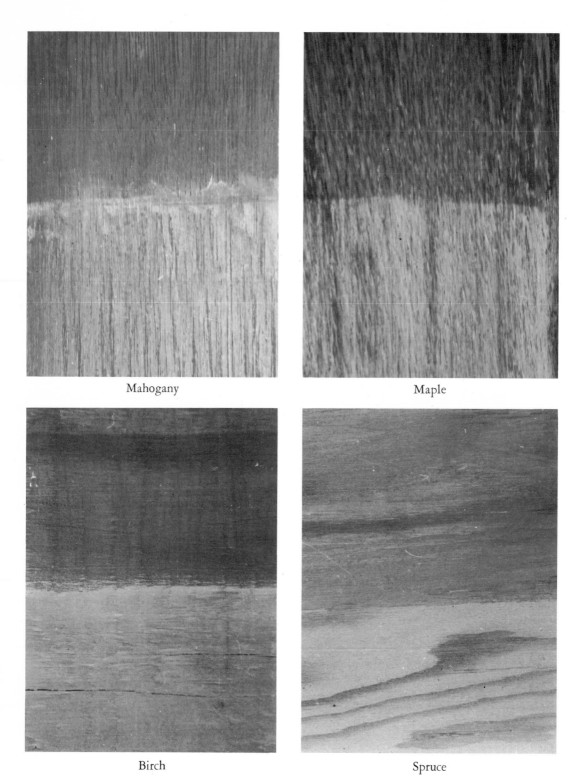

Mahogany　　　　　　　　　　Maple

Birch　　　　　　　　　　Spruce

Figure 12. These four different types of wood are stained to a darker color; then a lighter patina is applied. The top half of each piece of wood shows its initial stain. The bottom half shows the stain covered with the patina.

suited to patinas. The more open the grain of the wood, the more conspicuous will be the effect of the patina (Figure 12). On wood with a very close grain, the patina will have little chance to become imbedded in its texture; therefore the effect of the patina will be weaker. The tone of the wood will also determine in a large measure the effect of the patina. The darker the wood's tone and the lighter the patina, the more dramatic the contrast will be. Conversely, the closer the shade of the patina with that of the wood, the more delicate the effect. It stands to reason that neither of these extremes appears to be desirable; the first will produce a restless effect, the second simply will not be effective; we need something more moderate. Therefore, we shall try to achieve stronger contrasts between the color of the wood and its patina.

Step-by-Step Patina Procedure

Any dark-colored wood can be finished with a patina. Here is the procedure:

Step 1. Stain the wood to a desired color, and keep its tone rather dark. Remember that on a light surface the patina will not register well. Allow the acrylic paint, or the coffee solution, or whatever staining material you are using, to dry well.

Step 2. Mix the white acrylic gesso with umber acrylic (raw or burnt) to produce a medium gray color—neither too light, nor too dark. Thin the mixture with water to the consistency of milk.

Step 3. Brush the patina all over the surface of the wood; do not allow it to dry!

Step 4. Rub off the wet patina with a moist (not wet!) rag. Allow the patina to remain only in the crevices and grain of the wood's texture.

Step 5. When dry, polish the wood's surface with a fine carborundum paper. Effects of the patina on a variety of boards is seen in Figure 12.

Alternate Patina Method

An alternate method calls for spraying thin coats of lighter enamel colors on a darker, previously stained wood surface (see page 50). This method should only be used on modestly proportioned surfaces not exceeding the the size of a door, for example. Obviously the paneling of a room could not be very well treated with the help of an aerosol can.

This method is especially effective when used on an open-grained wood, such as mahogany. When using enamel colors in aerosol cans, spray in a fanning manner; hold the can at a distance of at least 12″ from the wood. To avoid clogging the grain of the wood do not use an excessive amount of spray.

3

Painting, Marbling, and Gilding Wood

We all know how drab wooden objects painted in one color can be. For example, think of kitchen furniture! Only some sort of an antique effect can relieve the uniform house painter's color of its all-pervading dullness. You can alleviate this monotony by superimposing another color on top of the solid, monotonous one. You can create uneven, spotted, or mottled effects characteristic of faded "antique" paint. There are two techniques you can use to create these "antique" effects: glazing and scumbling. A *glaze* is a darker transparent color applied to a lighter, underlying color. A scumble is just the reverse—a lighter, semitransparent color resting on top of a darker surface. The color used for a glaze should never be mixed with white, because white will destroy its transparency. On the contrary, white should always be mixed with every color used as a scumble. In this way, the scumble will be semitransparent when it is used as a thin film and will be able to partially cover its darker underlying surface.

The Glaze

When referring to the light, underlying base color of a glaze only acrylic yellow oxide can be used without an admixture of white. Other colors such as red, brown (umber), black, green, and blue are dark and will have to receive enough white to produce light pastel hues. Thus red will turn into pink, brown into a warm gray, black into a cold gray, blue into a pale blue, and green into a jade-like color or light bluish green, depending

Figure 13. The specific technique called glazing produces the interesting pattern that changes this ordinary wooden stool into a decorative piece of furniture. A burnt umber glaze is applied over a yellow oxide underpaint.

on the tint of the particular green. None of these colors should be thinned with water; use them full strength.

Once this underlying pastel color has dried, the thin, dark transparent color of the glaze should be brushed on top of it. It can be any color—burnt siena, umber, black, phthalo blue, or green—greatly diluted with a mixture of half water and half acrylic medium.

For example, your underlying surface could be yellow oxide with a glaze of black, green, blue or umber; the resulting color effect would be green. If your underlying surface were pink, you could use a glaze of phthalo blue or green; the resulting effect would then be a blend of both these colors. If you use a burnt siena or umber, your resulting effect would be a warm reddish color. If your underlying surface is blue or green you can use a burnt siena glaze. This seems to be the only combination yielding a truly attractive color effect.

Step-by-Step Glazing of a Stool

In this (Figure 13) and the following demonstration (Figure 14) I'll be using simple, unpainted wooden stools to illustrate techniques. The application of a glaze is described in the following:

Step 1. Paint the entire surface of the stool smoothly with yellow oxide acrylic, using a utility brush. Be sure to mix your yellow oxide with white to reduce its strength to an even lighter pastel. Allow your underlying color to dry.

Step 2. Thin the acrylic color to be used for the glaze, in this case burnt umber, to a liquid consistency. Thin the color with a mixture consisting of one half water and one half acrylic medium.

Step 3. Instead of applying the glaze color with a utility brush all over the dry acrylic surface and then texturing it with a sponge or cheesecloth, you can also apply the glaze with a piece of sturdy paper cut the same size as the stool's top. Cover the piece of paper generously with the thinned burnt umber. Now wet the top of the stool with water and press the paint-covered paper onto the stool's top. Lift and press down repeatedly.

Step 4. Upon drying, give the stool's top a high sheen with common floor varnish. However, the stool's legs and rungs could remain in the flat finish that the yellow acrylic oxide has imparted to them, or they can also be varnished.

Figure 14. This stool has been finished with a technique called scumbling. White acrylic gesso produces the scumble on a ground of phthalo blue acrylic.

The Scumble

The underlying dark color in a scumble—red oxide, burnt siena, umber, black, phthalo blue, or green—should be used without the admixture of white and without dilution. Any color used on top of the dark, underlying one should be mixed with white to show up against the darker background. Then, this second color should be considerably thinned with a mixture of one half water and one half acrylic medium. Spray enamels can also be used for the underlying colors.

Here are some possible color combinations that could be used. Your underlying surface could be a solid (opaque) color of red oxide. For scumbling on top you could use thin washes of pink, blue, green, or gray. On a black underpainting you could use pink or gray. On blue and green you could use scumbles of the same colors, thus graying down the original, underlying color.

While a scumble color is still wet, you can press a piece of cloth or sponge into it to produce the mottled effect characteristic of some antique polychromy. If your wood surface possesses knots, these must first be shellacked in order to prevent them from *bleeding* (appearing through the overpainting).

Step-by-Step Scumbling of a Stool

Once again, I have used a common, unpainted wooden stool for my demonstration (Figure 14) which proceeds as follows:

Step 1. Cover the entire surface of the stool with a dark, acrylic color; in this case it is phthalo blue. Then, mix any desired color with white for the scumble. This makes the scumble color appear much lighter than the surface upon which it will be applied.

Step 2. After the underlying color has dried, you can scumble color all over it with a utility brush. However, in this case you can use an alternate method of applying a scumble. Take a sturdy piece of paper big enough to cover the entire top of the stool; cover this piece of paper with white acrylic gesso thinned with water.

Step 3. After I moisten the now-dry surface of the stool, I press the paint-covered paper onto the stool's top. Then, I reverse the paper and press its dry side onto the stool's top. I lift the paper and press down again. This produces a more interesting pattern.

Figure 15. Here is a view of the entire stool whose top is seen in Figure 14. Just like the stool shown in Figure 13, its legs and rungs remain in a mat finish produced by the initial acrylic underpaint; this mat finish provides a contrast to the glossy tops.

Step 4. Varnish the stool's top with any common floor varnish, not its rungs and legs (Figure 15).

Marbling

Marbling is an intriguing manipulation of paint which produces the most enchanting decorative effects; even an amateur can use this technique. The term "marbling" refers to the imitation of those colorful patterns found in richly veined marble.

The practice of "marbling" wooden surfaces existed centuries ago; it was a response to a prevailing fashion, not just a way to make a cheap substitution. In fact, painted "marble" was more highly valued than the genuine article. In the late eighteenth century, the passion for marbling was so widespread that marble effects were applied to objects where they were completely out of place—on doors, for example. It was not only the elegant world which indulged in such decoration; it was also widely used in the homes of peasants. I must, however, quickly add that all decorative and utilitarian objects in common use before the advent of the machine age were always in the best of taste. Today, of course, these "antique" household objects are sought after by collectors.

To return to marbling, on what objects could this technique be applied to enhance their appeal? Chairs, shelves, table and stool tops, boxes, cabinets, frames, lighting fixtures, in short a great variety of utilitarian, as well as decorative, items made of wood can benefit from this technique.

Once more I shall have to point out that the processes described in this book have been devised so that amateurs (who have no special skills in using brushes) can use them. Marbling that involves brush manipulation is fully dealt with in my book *Restoring and Preserving Antiques*. Here I'll employ different methods from those mentioned in the earlier book, but ones that, nevertheless, lead to very rewarding results.

Most of the examples of marbling presented in the color plates carry a spray enamel foundation. Some will be finished in acrylic colors applied on top of this enamel foundation. Some will be executed in acrylics throughout. The practicability of one method *vis à vis* another will be discussed in each case.

The Nature and Use of Spray Enamels

These enamel paints come in aerosol cans and are sold under various trade names such as Jet Spray (Behlen Bro.), Krylon, Blair, etc. Since the names of the various colors are not standardized among the various manufacturers, I shall simply refer to them by the general nomenclatures such as: white, yellow, red, brown, blue, green, black. Besides these, there are the metallic sprays such as silver, aluminum (these are almost identical), bright gold, copper, and other metallic tints. These sprays offer an easy execution of endless combinations of colors and textural effects and also provide a most pleasurable activity.

The spray enamels produce colors that have a high gloss. They eject in a fine spray and dry rapidly, providing a little of them is used at one time. When thicker films of the enamel are piled up, drying is considerably delayed. Thin or heavy application depends on the distance from which the spray is ejected, and, of course, the length of time of application. When holding the aerosol can at a distance of less than 8", too much of the paint settles at one spot on the surface; therefore, it is advisable not to come too close to the object to be sprayed. If the distance is quite far—15" or 20" away—the droplets become bigger and cover the surface with less density, which is not necessarily a detriment. It all depends on the nature of the effects you wish to produce.

The enamels have a moderate covering power when used sparingly; the underlying color disappears only when the minute droplets merge. This circumstance is particularly advantageous, inasmuch as it can produce the effects of a glaze or a scumble. Actually, a surface solidly covered with enamel paint (except for the metallic ones) is uninteresting, simply because of its unvarying monotony.

Marbling with Spray Enamels

As mentioned, marbling denotes the production of effects that simulate the appearance of colorful surfaces found in richly grained, polished marble. The simplest way to achieve such effects is by using spray enamels. The principle of the procedure is to first provide a solid surface of a certain color. On top of this foundation, another enamel is sprayed lightly, so that the underlying surface is not completely covered. Such superimposition of colors creates opalescent effects characteristic of highly polished marbles. The further away you hold the aerosol can when spraying, the larger some of the droplets will appear, often adding to the variety of textural effects.

In the color plates on pages 51 and 52, this use of spray enamels is seen. A complete discussion of the step-by-step procedure used in each plate follows:

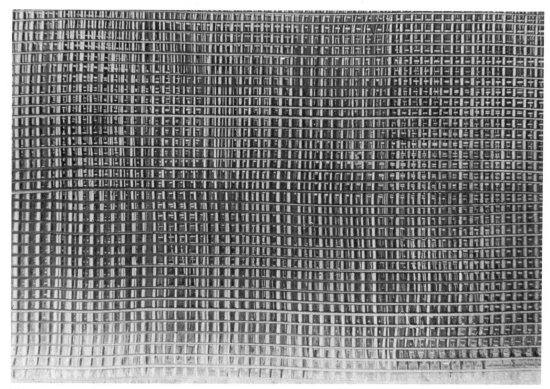

Figure 16. Besides creating variations in color, the technique of glazing can also produce variations in texture. The striated pattern shown here is produced by pulling a rubber comb across, as well as up and down, a wet phthalo green glaze that has been applied to a light gray surface. See page 59 for a color view of this pattern used on a chest of drawers.

Marbling Effects on a Black Enamel Foundation

In the color plates on pages 51 and 52 gold and silver metallic spray enamels are used. The reason for the black enamel foundation is that both these metallic sprays are more effective when contrasted with a dark ground. If the metallic appearance gets too solid, hence monotonous, black can be applied—with greatest economy—on top of the metallic spray to variegate the surface.

In examples C and D on page 51 the same idea prevails. A solidly colored surface is avoided by marblizing it. In example C, red and white spray enamel is sparsely applied over the same black enamel foundation. In example D, both white and a darker enamel are alternately sprayed lightly over the black foundation. The aerosol can should be held at a distance of about 10″ or more from the surface under treatment. The spray should be emitted in a kind of a "dusting" fashion achieved by moving the can back and forth like a fan.

Spraying of different colors can be done in rapid succession. However, if quick drying appears to be desirable, thinness of these applications is essential. A few minutes' time should be allowed between applications, and piling up of the paint should be avoided. As mentioned, a thin application of color will dry at once, but an appreciably thicker layer will require many hours to solidify completely.

Textural Effects with Spray Enamels

In examples A and B of the color plate on page 52, the same technique is used as in the foregoing, except that on example A the spraying is done from a considerable distance. Red and white spray enamels are applied from a distance of 30″; hence the larger size of the droplets. In example B, black and yellow enamels are sprayed interchangeably over a foundation of yellow enamel.

But in example C the procedure is quite different. Here a (dry) foundation of gold and silver enamels are thoroughly wetted with a soapy water. (Because of its surface tension, water will not smoothly go over the glassy surface of enamel unless conditioned by soap or a detergent.) Next, black enamel is sprayed onto the wet surface and immediately textured with a wet paper towel. *Because of the quick drying of the enamel colors, the speed of this operation is essential.* The interesting patterns thus produced are due to the incompatibility of the enamel paint and water. (Text continued on page 65.)

Wood Stains. Softwoods can be stained with such everyday products as coffee and tea. Starting at the top, tea is used as the staining agent for the first two light yellowish stains. Coffee produces a darker brown stain as seen in the two bottom rows.

A. Sky-blue spray enamel over a mahogany-colored stain.

B. Bright red spray enamel over a black stain.

C. White spray enamel over an ochre stain.

D. Gray spray enamel over a black stain.

E. Yellow spray enamel over a black stain.

Patinas on Wood. The patinas shown here are produced by spraying lighter colored enamels over darker stained wood surfaces.

A. Gold spray enamel applied sparingly to a black enamel foundation.

B. Gold and silver spray enamels applied interchangeably to a black enamel foundation.

C. White and red spray enamels applied interchangeably to a black enamel foundation.

D. White spray enamel applied sparingly to a black enamel foundation.

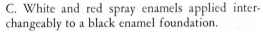

Marbling on Enamels. The technique of marbling can produce a variety of effects depending on the different enamel colors you choose.

A. Red and white spray enamels applied interchangeably to a red enamel foundation.

B. Black and yellow spray enamels applied sparingly to a yellow enamel foundation.

C. Black enamel sprayed over a silver and gold enamel foundation that has been covered with soapy water and textured with a wet paper towel.

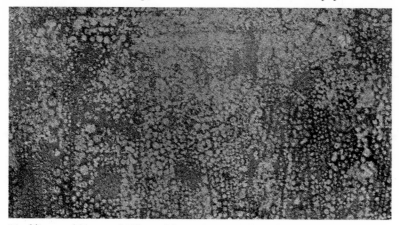

Marbling and Textural Effects. The technique of marbling can also produce interesting textural as well as pictorial effects.

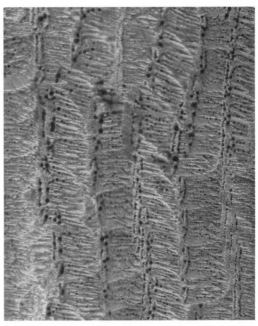

A. White enamel foundation with black acrylic thinly applied and textured with wet paper towel.

B. White enamel foundation with phthalo blue acrylic applied and textured with a soft-hair

C. Yellow enamel foundation with burnt umber acrylic (diluted with water) textured with a sponge.

D. Yellow enamel foundation with burnt umber acrylic textured with a rubber comb.

Spray Enamels and Acrylic Paints. Here are four examples of the different types of textures you can produce with spray enamels and acrylic paints.

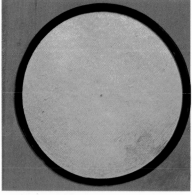

A. Red spray enamel foundation with gold enamel circle.

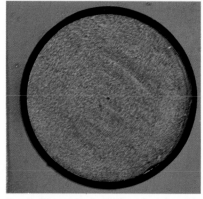

B. Gold enamel circle glazed with burnt umber and textured with cheesecloth.

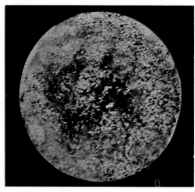

C. Black enamel foundation; silver enamel circle glazed with black acrylic and textured with cheesecloth.

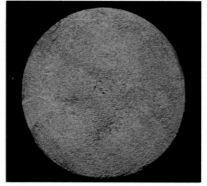

D. Silver circle glazed with a phthalo green acrylic and textured with cheesecloth.

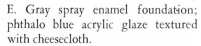

E. Gray spray enamel foundation; phthalo blue acrylic glaze textured with cheesecloth.

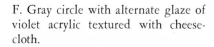

F. Gray circle with alternate glaze of violet acrylic textured with cheese-cloth.

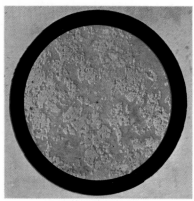

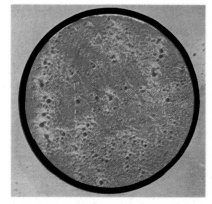

Circular Designs with Templets. A paper templet is used to produce all these simple, circular designs. Metallic sprays are used to fill in the circles and black marker is used to delineate them.

1. Black spray enamel foundation.

1. Yellow spray enamel foundation.

2. Red and white spray enamels used interchangeably on the circle.

2. Burnt siena acrylic glaze applied to circle and textured with cheesecloth.

3. The area around the circle marbled with phthalo green, blue, and white acrylic textured with cheesecloth.

3. With templet protecting the circle, outlying areas sprayed with black enamel.

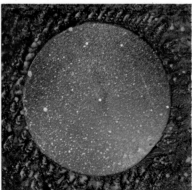

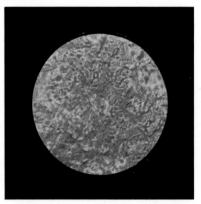

Designing with Templets. A paper templet is used to produce this simple design which can be varied in endless ways by using different colors and texturing materials.

1. Cadmium red spray enamel foundation.

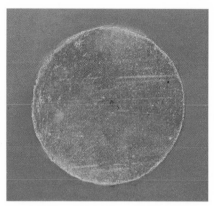

4. Gold enamel sprayed on circle with paper templet protecting rest of design.

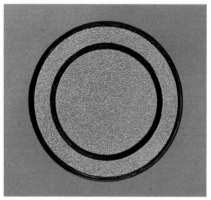

2. Outer and inner circles drawn with compass that is fitted with a, nylon-tipped marker.

3. The segments connected with diagonal lines.

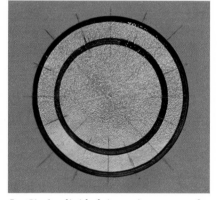

5. Circle divided into sixteen equal segments with a pencil.

6. The eight newly created triangles filled in with black marker, producing a star.

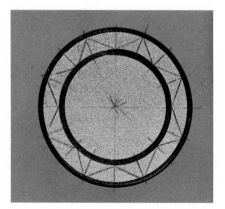

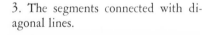

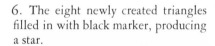

Star Inscribed in Circle. This interesting star-within-a-circle design is easily executed with templets, spray enamels, and acrylic paints.

A. Light gray acrylic foundation.

B. Inner rectangle glazed with cadmium red acrylic textured with wet cheesecloth; outside rectangle glazed with phthalo green acrylic textured with paper towel.

C. Inner rectangle glazed with cadmium red acrylic and textured with a soft-hair brush; outer rectangle glazed with ultramarine blue acrylic textured with wet cheesecloth.

D. Inner rectangle glazed with cadmium red acrylic textured with a piece of wet cloth; outer rectangle glazed with greatly diluted ultramarine blue acrylic textured with a soft sponge.

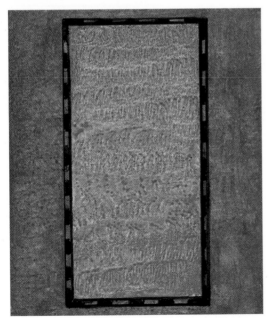

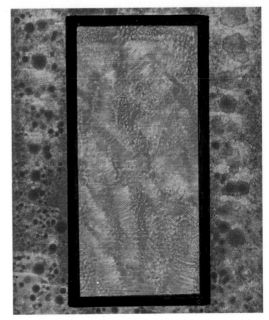

Designs with Masking Tape. Here masking tape rather than paper templets is used to separate color areas while paint is applied.

Eight-Pronged Star. The delineation of this star design is explained in step-by-step diagrams on page 75. After a mixture of yellow oxide and white acrylic is painted on as a foundation, a templet is used to cover a circular area. The surface surrounding the circular templet is painted with burnt umber acrylic. While still wet, the burnt umber is textured with a soft sponge. Two additional templets are cut to cover both the area surrounding the circle and the star itself. The exposed area within the circle (and around the star) is glazed with burnt umber acrylic which is textured with a dry sponge to produce a burlwood effect. The star is divided into segments which are alternately colored with black marker or left to reveal the light yellow of the original foundation paint.

Refinished Chest of Drawers. The handsome design used on this piece employs both the techniques of marbling and glazing. See pages 81–85 for the step-by-step procedures.

Cabinet. Marbling, also used on this piece of furniture, allows you to use simple geometric designs and still produce varied effects. See pages 87–89 for the step-by-step procedures.

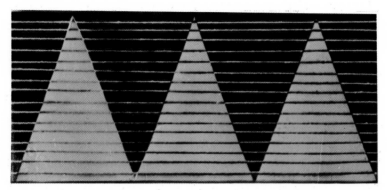

Refinished Top of Small Bench. Although the design appears to be quite intricate, only two colors and paper templets are used to produce it. This exciting design receives its stripes from the interesting use of string. See page 93 for the step-by-step procedure.

Refinished Top of Small Table. Both spray enamels and acrylic paints are used to produce the simple but effective geometric design for the table's top. See page 91 for the step-by-step procedure.

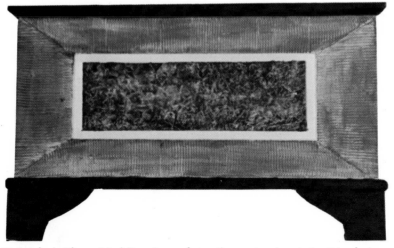

Refinished Chest. Marbling is used on the center insert in this design. On the outer rectangle notice the striated effects produced by a rubber comb run through the wet glaze. See page 95 for the procedure.

Refinished Door. The gold spray enamel used on the moldings of this door serves to enhance the geometric design. See page 97 for the step-by-step procedure.

Refinished Highboy. Glazes, such as the burnt siena glaze used on the front of each drawer, can be textured with many different materials; in this case a crumpled, dry piece of paper towel is used. See page 99 for the step-by-step procedure.

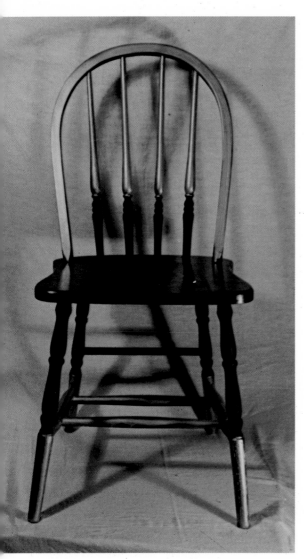

Refinished Chair (Detail).

Refinished Chair. After the entire chair is painted in black acrylic, gold spray enamel is used on the back, rods, and legs. Marbling is used on the chair's seat. See page 101 for the step-by-step procedure.

Patinas on Metal. (Above) Patinas on metals are produced with chemical solutions that actually cause chemical changes in the compositions of the metals. From right to left: a copper vase with a blue-green patina; a brass candlestick also with a blue-green patina; and another copper vase with brown-yellow-green patina. See pages 122–124 for the step-by-step procedures.

Decorative Objects. (Right) These three wooden objects have been finished in various ways. From left to right: a lamp base glazed with phthalo blue acrylic over a white and gray enamel foundation; a candlestick holder marbled with gold and silver spray enamels on a black spray enamel foundation; and a lamp base marbled with red enamel on a black enamel foundation. See pages 65–67 for the step-by-step procedures.

(Text continued from page 48.)

For example, on a black foundation white, yellow, or red can be used in the manner described. On a white foundation, green, blue, yellow, or red will do well. On a green or blue fundation, white, red, or yellow could produce striking effects.

Although a wet paper towel is used for texturing in example C (page 52), other materials can be used for texturing as well, such as cheesecloth, sponges, and some coarse textiles. These texturing materials must always be quite wet, or else they will attach themselves to the sticky surface.

Step-by-Step Marbling of a Candlestick Holder

This candlestick holder is made of wood (on the far left of Figure 17). When ordering any object from a woodturning shop, you should have it very well sanded. It is very easy to provide a perfectly smooth surface when working on a lath, but to smooth a richly configured surface by hand is quite tedious, often requiring excessive labor. The completely refinished candlestick holder can be seen in color on page 64. The marbling proceeds as follows:

Step 1. Spray the wooden holder with black enamel. When the enamel is dry, rub it with very fine steel wool. Spray again with black enamel. This will produce an extra smooth surface.

Step 2. Spray lightly with gold enamel. Let the holder dry.

Step 3. Spray with silver enamel, holding the aerosol can at some distance from the holder so as to produce stronger textural effects. After such treatment the candlestick holder does not require any further improvement of its glossy surface.

Step-by-Step Marbling of Two Lamp Bases

With the lamp base shown in the center of Figure 17 my intention is to simulate the appearance of a certain mineral aggregate—one that is black in color with finely interspersed red particles. The technique of marbling can help me achieve this effect. The completed lamp base can be seen in color on page 64. The procedure follows:

Step 1. Spray the entire wooden lamp base with black enamel.

Step 2 When the black enamel has dried, spray with red enamel. The intensity of red dots will increase as you move the aerosol can further

Figure 17. The decorative objects shown here from left to right are: a wooden candlestick holder finished with gold and silver metallic spray enamels on a black spray enamel foundation; a wooden lamp base finished with black and red spray enamels; and a wooden lamp base finished with a phthalo blue glaze on a white and gray spray enamel foundation. The finished objects can be seen in color on page 64.

away from the surface. This process may have to be repeated until a satisfactory interspersion of black and red dots is achieved. If desired, a more lively effect will result by using orange instead of the red color.

I use a different treatment in decorating the lamp base seen on the right in Figure 17. The foundation, just as in the former, is provided by spray enamel, in this case, of a light gray color. On it, in an irregular manner, I spray a white enamel. The reason for this preliminary procedure is that when glazing such a variegated surface, I can obtain a more interesting effect. To remind the reader, when I refer to *glazing* I mean a transparent or semitransparent application of paint. Such treatment will produce a porcelain-like effect. The procedure follows:

Step 1. Spray white and gray enamel in an interchanging irregular manner over the entire lamp base to provide a foundation.
Step 2. Rub the now enameled surface with very fine steel wool to remove its gloss.

Step 3. Brush water containing some detergent onto the surface of the lamp base. This is done to allow the subsequent application of acrylic glaze to go over the enameled surface smoothly.

Step 4. Apply a glaze of phthalo blue acrylic color to the surface. Texture the glaze with a wet sponge.

Step 5. When the glaze has dried, spray the surface with clear plastic spray.

Step-by-Step Gilding Technique

As mentioned in Chapter 1, although gilding with leaves is not very difficult, it requires a certain skill that a beginner might not have. In this procedure I shall be using wax gilt called "Treasure Gold Wax Gilt." The step-by-step procedure follows:

Step 1. The surface to be gilded should be polished to a perfect smoothness, and rendered nonabsorbent with the acrylic medium. The color of the surface is immaterial since the metallic substance will cover it completely.

Step 2. Take up a little of the wax gilt on a piece of cloth; rub it into the surface, and polish the gilt to a high gloss.

Step 3. Polish the gilt to a still higher gloss with a burnisher (see Figure 8). Burnishing not only increases the gloss, but it also fuses the minute particles of the metal to a solid mass.

Step 4. Allow the gilt to harden at least twenty-four hours. Next, if an "antique" effect appears to be desirable, coat the gilt with orange shellac. A still stronger effect can be created if a glaze of burnt umber acrylic color is used before applying the shellac. The burnt umber glaze should be textured with cheesecloth, then waxed and polished to a high gloss. If you wish to make the application mat, apply the gilt wax paste without subsequent polishing.

As to the use of silver, follow the same procedure, but here "antiquing" is inadvisable. A coat of white shellac or the acrylic medium will protect it; a soft-hair brush should be used to apply the shellac. Antique appearances can be simulated when using pewter colored paste. In all, the wax paste metallic applications are especially useful for repairing abrasions on existing gilded or silvered surfaces, as well as giving such surfaces new luster.

Metallic Spray Enamels

Gold, copper, silver, and aluminum spray enamels can be employed to create metallic finishes. A description of the step-by-step procedure follows:

Step 1. Make the surface to be treated as smooth as possible and render it nonabsorbent with acrylic medium. Here, too, its original color is immaterial.

Step 2. Spray the surface in the usual manner and build up a solid metallic surface.

Step 3. Allow the metallic coating to harden perfectly. This may take a few hours or more. You can "antique" a bright gold surface with orange shellac. Acrylic burnt umber glaze textured with cheesecloth can also be applied prior to the use of the shellac. In the case of copper spray enamel, glazing with burnt umber alone will suffice. Silver (or aluminum) can be glazed with raw umber. Unusual effects on silver can be produced with a phthalo green glaze.

Whenever acrylic colors are diluted with water, they will turn flat when dry. Therefore, if you are going to use these colors as finishes and you want them to be glossy, burnishing will be necessary. Burnishing will produce a gloss at once, but the agate or steel burnisher cannot be used very well on large surfaces. Hence, these large surfaces first should be brushed vigorously with a soft shoeshine brush, then waxed and polished to a high gloss.

4

Creating Designs and Textured Finishes

Of all the marbling processes the one that combines both spray enamels and acrylic paints offers the most varied effects, simply because, contrary to work with spray enamels, acrylic colors can be textured manually and without undue haste. Unless otherwise indicated, I shall be using in the forthcoming examples a spray enamel foundation and then texturing it with acrylic colors.

Texturing With Acrylics on Spray Enamel

An acrylic color, when applied on top of a solid spray enamel foundation, allows manipulation as long as it is wet; when wet it can be textured in various ways. Depending on the nature of the material used for texturing—cheesecloth, sponge, cloth (wet or dry)—and the manner of its employment, endless patterns and textural effects can be produced.

In the color plate on page 53 four examples of texturing with a combination of spray enamels and acrylics can be seen. In examples A and B of that color plate, the texturing as well as the coloring resemble some semi-precious stones. Example C closely approximates burlwood, and example D simulates a long-grained wood. The execution of these textures does not require any special skill. Simple twists and movements of the texturing tool will produce such patterns—as long as the acrylic paint remains wet.

Preparing Enameled Surfaces for Acrylic Paint

Enameled surfaces will not accept an acrylic overpaint especially when the acrylic is slightly diluted with water. This resistance can be overcome by rubbing an enameled surface with steel wool to remove its gloss. Soapy water applied to the enameled surface will also make the acrylic overpaint adhere to it. However, "using" soapy water does not mean just brushing it on the surface. To make the soapy water cover the enameled surface thoroughly, it is necessary to apply it vigorously and repeatedly until all trickling disappears.

You may now ask why you should use an enamel foundation at all? When examining the finished product, it becomes obvious that all colors appear to be more brilliant when they rest on enameled foundations. Moreover, there is no easier way to produce a perfectly even, flawless surface than to spray enamels from aerosol cans.

Should a particular acrylic finish of an enameled surface prove to be unsuccessful, just apply a new foundation on top of it and repeat the overpaint. As mentioned, removal of an undesirable acrylic finish can be done with lacquer thinner or with a paint remover, but these solvents will act on the enamel foundation as well. Hence, it is advisable to cover up an undesired overpaint (after rendering it smooth with polishing paper) with another, perhaps contrasting, acrylic color and pattern it in any manner described.

Finishes for Acrylic Overpaints

When dry, the acrylic overpaint will become flat. *To revamp its gloss and hence the depth of color, varnish the acrylic paint with acrylic medium.* On smaller surfaces a soft-hair brush can be used to apply the medium. On large surfaces, a soft-textured sponge will be more practical. Of course, a clear plastic spray instead of the acrylic medium can also be used to produce a glossy finish.

Creating Designs with Templets

A templet is basically a pattern used to create designs. For our purposes, paper templets will be used, but they are sometimes made in thin metal or wood. The templets should be cut out of a sturdy but not too stiff paper and attached to your surface by means of rubber cement (Quick Stick adhesive). Templets will protect areas that are to receive colors different from those you are painting on the adjoining areas; they work in the same way that masking tape does when you are painting straight lines. To emphasize particular designs and divide them into definite patterns, black outlines of varied widths can be produced by means of nylon-tipped or felt-tipped markers. These outlines can be straight which will call for the use of a ruler, or they can be circular, in which case the appropriate marker should be attached to a compass.

If you want decorations other than the overall patterns possible with spray enamels and acrylics, a templet (or templets) must be used to separate one part of your pattern, or design, from another, thus allowing them to be painted with different colors.

Constructing a Templet

As mentioned, a sturdy but soft paper should be used for the templet. First, draw the outlines of your design with a pencil. For the straight lines in your design, use a ruler; for the curves, use a circle. In Figures 4 and 6 of Chapter 1 two differently shaped blades appear on the X-Acto knives. For cutting along straight lines always use the pointed ones; for curves, use the curved ones. The paper should be cut on a smooth, hard surface such as cardboard.

Using a Templet

Figures 18 and 19 (opposite page) are diagrams of the two templets that I'll be describing in the following procedure. These two templets will allow you to produce a circle of a particular color on a ground of a different color. Needless to say, the basic procedure used to produce this relatively simple design can be modified and used to create very intricate ones, some of which will be discussed later in this chapter.

Step 1. Place templet I on area B and fasten the paper templet with Quick Stick adhesive.

Step 2. Spray area B (including the paper templet) with the desired color. The paper templet will protect the surface beneath it from the paint spray.

Step 3. After lifting templet I, the area beneath it (designated as area A) will appear in the original color of the surface. Depending on your design, you can leave area A in this untreated condition, or you can apply a different color to it. If you wish to make area A a different color, you will need another templet, called Templet II in Figure 19.

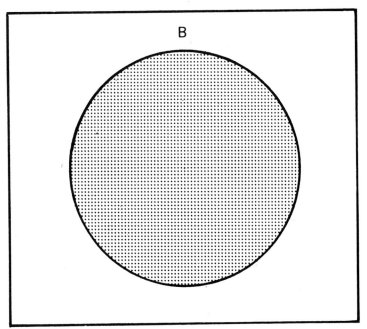

Figure 18. This paper templet allows you to use a spray enamel on Area B and, at the same time, protects the circular area in the center from the paint. When the templet is lifted off, the area beneath it (called Area A in Figure 19) will have the color of the original surface.

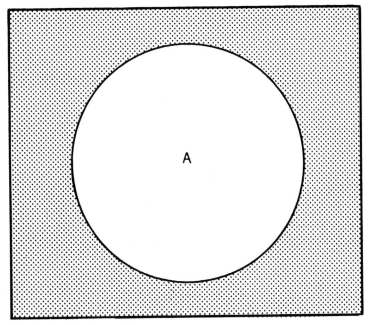

Figure 19. If you would like to apply a color to the circle (or Area A) that is different from the color of Area B, you will need a second templet to cover the area surrounding the circle.

Step 4. Place templet II on area B. This templet leaves the circular area, area A, unprotected. You may now apply a different color to this area with either a brush or spray.

Such templets as those described can be used to produce an infinite variety of color and textural combinations. See the color plates on pages 54, 55, and 56 for examples of such combinations produced from two such simple templets.

Delineating Borders

It is essential in every design that the borders between the color areas are firmly delineated. This requires not only exactness of a templet's borders, but also firm attachment of the templet to the surface of the object under treatment. For this attachment Quick Stick adhesive should be applied mainly to the edges of a templet. Allow the adhesive to become sticky; if wet, the attachment may become too firm. Should the adhesive become attached in spots to the surface, it can be removed by brushing lightly with kerosene. You should refrain from using strong solvents that may remove the enamel or acrylic paint from your surface.

When spraying your design it is quite important to hold the aerosol can directly above the templet. When held at an angle, the force of the spray may enter under the border of the templet, and consequently the outlines of the design may become diffused.

Metallic Applications and Their Patinas

Now you may ask why I have used patinas on the metallic applications in the color plate on page 54. The answer is that according to my experience, gathered from the study of antique, gilded objects, a warm brown color best simulates such an antique look. On the other hand, only black (with some brown added) can conjure up the look of an antique patina on silver. As for the phthalo green glaze on silver (example D in the color plate on page 54), it is simply the most effective coloration, although not suggestive of a particular patina. It is also important to provide colors such as those used in the color plate on page 54 with appropriate textures, and in all cases a wet cheesecloth seems best for the occasion.

In examples A through D of the color plate on page 54 only gold and sil-

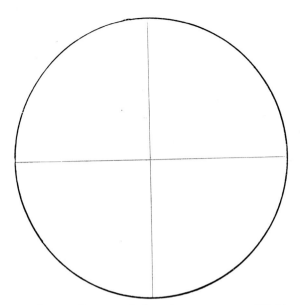

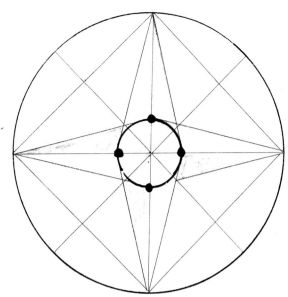

Step 1. Draw a circle using a compass. Divide this circle into four equal sections with a ruler.

Step 2. Divide the four sections in half, forming eight equal sections. Inscribing a square within the circle facilitates this division.

Step 3. With a smaller compass, draw a small circle within the main circle. This smaller circle helps to define the width of the prongs of the star.

Step 4. Draw a second, larger circle within the main circle. This second circle defines the width of the secondary prongs. Then, divide the prongs in half and alternately fill in the segments.

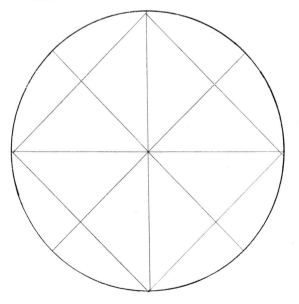

Figure 20. The construction of this star (which appears in color on page 58) is easier to make than its final appearance would indicate.

ver spray enamels are employed. However, gold and silver gilt (as well as other colored metallic wax compounds) could also be used.

The procedure is quite simple. Take a little of the wax-gold compound on your finger or a piece of cheesecloth and move it over the edge of the templet. There is no need to attach the templet to produce an accurately demarked border as must be done when using spray gold because your finger holds the templet firmly in place. When solidified (this will take a day or two), the wax gilding can be burnished to increased its gloss. Antiquing of such applications in the usual manner with the acrylic colors is also possible. Such gilt applications can be protected with acrylic medium after the gilt hardens completely; this may take several days.

Delineating with Markers

Black markers have been used to create the borders around the colored fields in the color plates on pages 54–56. Different brands of markers react differently under various solvents; some are even water-soluble. Such water-soluble markers will not permit the use of an acrylic overpaint; some dry instantly on totally nonabsorbent grounds; and some remain moist on such grounds for hours. Moreover, gold, as well as silver, enamel may not readily accept some markers. Their black ink may "trickle" on the metallic surface, and repeated efforts will be required to make such markers stick. A mild solvent such as paint thinner brushed lightly on the metallic surface will make it more receptive to the markers. Remember that all designs should be done on well-hardened metallic surfaces, and for all demarcations only a soft pencil, such as 6B, should be used. Even on a hard surface you should avoid using any pencil pressure that would leave indelible marks on it.

Markers can be used to create both straight and curved borders. When markers are used with a straight edge, such as a ruler, geometric shapes can be delineated accurately. When inserted in a compass, markers can produce perfect circular borders.

Using Masking Tape in Designs

In the color plates on pages 54, 55 and 56 paper templets are used. In the color plate on page 57, however, only masking tape is employed for limiting the color areas along straight lines. The rectangular patterns seen in this color plate are well suited for decorating objects such as cabinets, chests, doors, etc. Although these patterns may appear to be complex, their execution is extremely simple. Here, the "magic" of masking tape and mechanical means of texturing replace manual dexterity and professional skill.

In contrast to the preceding examples, only acrylic colors are used on the patterns seen in the color plate on page 57. In this color plate the foundation color is light gray. A gray can be best produced by mixing white acrylic gesso with umber and phthalo blue acrylic. Depending on the predominance of the brown or the blue color, the gray will be warmer or cooler, respectively. But regardless of its tonality, the gray must be light enough to give a sparkle to the color superimposed on it.

Next, masking tape is used to square up and separate the various segments before coloring them. Attaching masking tape along straight lines is difficult. Therefore, first a guiding straight line should be drawn with a pencil and a ruler; then masking tape should be placed along it. To protect the rest of the design areas, it is best to cover them with a piece of heavy paper or cardboard.

Correcting Designs

While executing various designs, slips may occur requiring correction. As mentioned, traces of Quick Stick adhesive can be removed from an enameled surface with kerosene. Although kerosene's dissolving action is weaker than that of any other petroleum solvent, excessive rubbing should be avoided, because enamel applications are vulnerable to petroleum solvents and alcohol.

Minor corrections such as retouching can be made by releasing some of the spray enamel into a small container; a round sable brush can be used to apply the paint. The most effective cleaning agent for cleaning enamel color from brushes is acetone. Of course, corrections can be made by repeated sprays of enamels, or reapplications of acrylics.

Before they solidify, acrylic applications can be easily removed from an enameled surface with water. Dry acrylic paint yields to benzene, lacquer thinner, acetone, or paint removers.

Black marker can be wiped off with kerosene—as long as it is still fresh. For old, dried marker ink use stronger solvents such as lacquer thinner or acetone. It is also well to remember that the dye of many of the markers will bleed through an acrylic color. Therefore, such marks should be eliminated before beginning any overpainting. Moreover, the dye in some markers is water soluble, which makes them vulnerable when varnished with acrylic medium. Hence, surfaces on which markers have been used should be protected with clear plastic spray.

Enameled surfaces can be protected with acrylic medium and/or wax. Only paste wax should be used, because some of the liquid waxes may contain strong solvents that can affect the underlying enamel color.

5

Refinishing and Antiquing Furniture

Much of the furniture dating from about the fifteenth and well into the middle of the nineteenth century was either carved, inlaid, painted, or decorated with ornaments. Painted furniture was predominantly of rustic or provincial origin, but no matter which class of society it served, such furniture had great charm and beauty. Because of my self-imposed limitations in regard to the techniques used, I shall be decorating the furniture in this chapter with designs of a geometric nature such as those developed in Chapter 4.

Now your task will be restoration of pieces of ordinary furniture, or rather their finishes (for carpentry is not on our program), that have lost their one-time appearance and are now in need of a more or less complete refinishing. These pieces are not costly "antiques" such as a pair of Louis XIV chairs. The refinishing you will do does not require any professional skill. Therefore, you should not try your hand at reconditioning *bona fide* antiques. However, the acrylic colors in conjunction with spray enamels, and the techniques developed in this book should allow the serious craftsman to *begin* to venture into the restoration of genuine antiques—especially after studying my book, *Restoring and Preserving Antiques,* where all the fine points of this art are discussed.

General Preparation

You will probably have to start from scratch with any piece of furniture you choose to refinish. This will involve some basic task, such as first using paint remover (providing that old paint or varnish still cling to your piece). Next, deep holes must be filled in with wood putty and minor cracks with acrylic modeling paste. Finally, the whole piece must be smoothed down with sandpaper.

Providing a Base Coat

The next step is to provide your piece with an overall coat of paint—a sort of *foundation coat*. Using your tube paint for an overall coat (or coats) of paint would be extravagant—and pointless—because the acrylic house paints will do as well. However, these paints must be thinned to a consistency that will not leave brushmarks. Because of their thin consistency, several layers of paint will be needed to provide a solid foundation.

As to the color of this foundation paint, it is best to keep it on the light side—a light gray, beige, yellow, and on some occasion even white. In certain cases, there will also be a need for a dark foundation on which light-colored effects may be applied.

Selecting a Design

Before undertaking any decoration of a complex nature, you should make sketches and give consideration to the most effective design.

The question now arises as to what patterns and ornaments you can use to decorate your furniture. In the following demonstrations, the designs I employ have been taken from the ornamentation used on predominantly rustic furniture found in Austria, Bavaria, Bohemia, Hungary, and the southern Tyrol in the eighteenth and early nineteenth centuries. However, I have used only decorations with strictly geometric patterns, because I feel that floral motifs and more complex designs are too difficult for the average beginner.

In this chapter, I shall discuss the step-by-step refinishing process for several pieces of furniture. In each case, I have provided illustrations of the pieces before they were refinished. The completed, refinished pieces of furniture can be seen in color on pages 59–64.

Step-by-Step Refinishing of a Chest of Drawers

On page 81 you can see the chest in the "raw," before refinishing. First, I remove the original, badly deteriorated paint and repair the major

Chest of Drawers, Before Refinishing. Here is the wooden chest of drawers in its "raw" state with most of its old paint removed. Before painting on the various designs, a coat of pale yellow acrylic was applied to the entire piece.

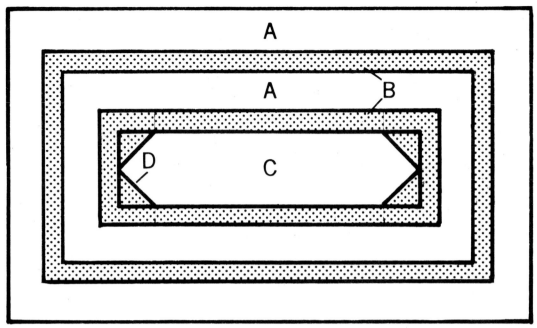

Chest of Drawers, Diagram for Top. The various areas of the design have been painted in the following colors: (A) pink marbling produced from cadmium red acrylic; (B) opaque brown-red produced from black and red acrylics. (C) phthalo green glaze striated with a rubber comb; and (D) black marker.

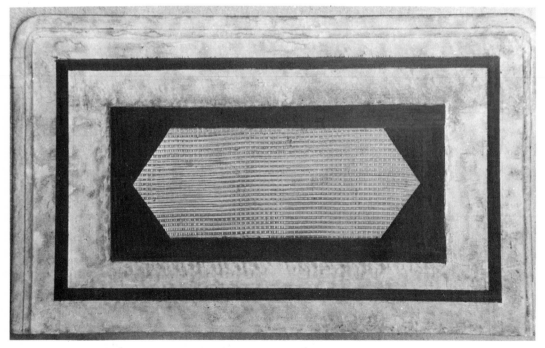

Chest of Drawers, Refinished Top. Here is the top of the chest of drawers refinished according to the diagram shown above. See page 59 for a color view of the entire chest of drawers.

scratches. Next, I apply an initial coat of pale yellow acrylic paint to the entire chest. I follow this with two additional coats. Then, I proceed with the refinishing as shown in the diagrams of the top, front, and side of the chest seen on pages 81–85. The materials required for this refinishing are cadmium red, phthalo green, black, and red oxide acrylic colors; masking tape; a rubber comb; and a sponge. I shall begin by describing the refinishing of the chest's top (see diagram, page 82):

Step 1. When the final coat of yellow acrylic has dried, glaze surface A with cadmium red acrylic following the glazing procedure described in Chapter 3. This should produce the look of an opalescent pink marble.

Step 2. Secure the borders around area B with masking tape and then fill in area B with opaque red-brown, produced from mixing both black and red oxide acrylic paints.

Step 3. Cover surface C with phthalo green. While the acrylic is still wet, create a striated texture on it by dragging a rubber comb across its surfaces as described in Chapter 4, Figure 16.

The front of the chest is treated as follows (see diagram, page 84):

Step 1. Cover the squares of the handle, area C, with masking tape.

Step 2. After applying a phthalo green glaze, striate the still wet glaze with a rubber comb.

Step 3. Remove the masking tape from surface C and place it around the borders of that area.

Step 4. Marble the entire uncovered surface of area C with a glaze of cadmium red.

Step 5. When area C is dry, color the segments of area D with black using the nylon-tipped marker for contouring and the felt marker for coloring the larger surfaces.

Step 6. Paint surfaces A solidly with red-brown acrylic. For the side view, the procedure will be identical with that used on the front (see diagram, page 85). The masking tape is used only to secure the borders of the red-brown areas. These are painted last.

As for the marbling procedures, they should be different so as to produce contrasting textural effects. Thus, a sponge can be used in place of the cheesecloth (or any other material) to create interesting and varied textural effects.

Chest of Drawers, Diagram for Front. (Right) The various areas of the design have been painted in the following colors: (A) opaque brown-red acrylic; (B) phthalo green glaze, striated with a rubber comb; (C) pink marbling produced from cadmium red acrylic; and (D) black marker.

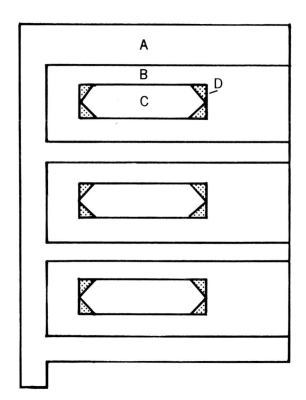

Chest of Drawers, Refinished Front. (Below) Here is the front of the chest refinished according to the diagram.

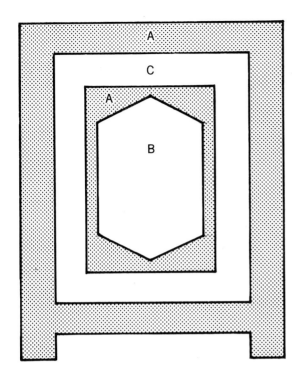

Chest of Drawers, Diagram for Side. The various areas of the design have been painted in the following colors: (A) opaque brown-red acrylic; (B) phthalo green glaze; (C) pink marbling produced from cadmium red acrylic.

Chest of Drawers, Refinished Side. This view shows the side of the chest of drawers refinished according to the diagram on the left.

Step-by-Step Refinishing of a Cabinet

The initial condition of this cabinet is seen on page 87. As with the chest of drawers, I apply an overall coat of yellow acrylic after the major scratches have been repaired. I follow this coat by two additional coats. The materials required to produce the decorations on this piece are: burnt umber, phthalo green, chromium oxide green, and black acrylic color; gold spray enamel; masking tape; a sponge; cheesecloth; black marker; and a paper templet. A description of the step-by-step procedure used in finishing the cabinet's top follows (see diagram, page 87):

Step 1. Marble surface A with a glaze of burnt umber acrylic, using the technique described in Chapter 3.

Step 2. Marble surface C with phthalo green acrylic. Neither surface B nor surface D needs to be protected with masking tape, because the opaque color of B (in this case a dark green mixed from chromium oxide green acrylic and black acrylic) and the opaque gold spray enamel will cover the underlying colors.

Step 3. Secure the borders around surface B with masking tape and paint surface B with the opaque green color.

Step 4. Place a rectangular paper templet on surface C which has been covered with phthalo green. Spray the now-exposed surface D with gold enamel spray.

Step 5. Outline the gold circle with black marker. Insert the marker in a large compass to facilitate an even line (see Figure 3, Chapter 1).

The front of the cabinet is treated as follows (see diagram, page 88):

Step 1. Marble surface B with burnt umber acrylic. Surface A will receive a dark opaque green; therefore you do not have to be concerned about going over its borders.

Step 2. Protect surface A, next to the center panel, all around with masking tape. Marble surface C with phthalo green acrylic.

Step 3. Place a rectangular paper templet, with a circle cut from its center, on surface C. Spray the open circle D with gold enamel.

Step 4. With a black marker outline circle D as you did in the chest of drawers.

Cabinet, Before Refinishing. The initial condition of the cabinet is seen here. Notice that most of its old paint has been removed as well as the knobs for its two doors.

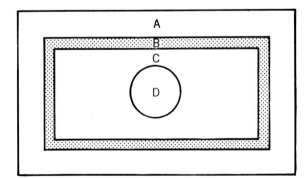

Cabinet, Diagram for Top. The various areas of the design have been painted in the following colors: (A) burnt umber acrylic glaze over yellow oxide acrylic foundation; (B) opaque dark green acrylic; (C) phthalo green acrylic marbling; and (D) gold spray enamel.

Cabinet, Refinished Top. Here is the top completely refinished according to the diagram. See page 60 for a color view of the entire cabinet.

Cabinet, Diagram for Front. (Right) The various areas of the design have been painted in the following colors: (A) opaque dark green acrylic; (B) burnt umber marbling; (C) phthalo green acrylic marbling; and (D) gold spray enamel.

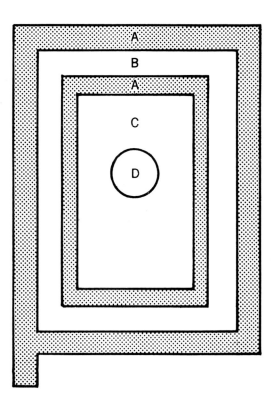

Cabinet, Refinished Front. (Below) Here is the front completely refinished according to the diagram.

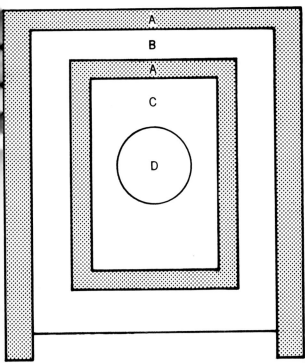

Cabinet, Diagram for Side. The various areas of the design have been painted in the following colors: (A) opaque dark green acrylic; (B) burnt umber marbling; (C) phthalo green acrylic marbling; and (D) gold spray enamel.

Cabinet, Refinished Side. Here is the side completely refinished according to the diagram.

The finishing of the cabinet's side follows the identical procedure used for its front.

Regarding the gilding of the circles, if desired, they could be antiqued with the umber acrylic color, using cheesecloth or a piece of sponge for texturing. However, if you prefer to use wax gilt, it can serve this purpose just as well. By moving your finger or a piece of cheesecloth (dipped previously in the wax-gold compound) over the edges of the paper templet around the cut-out, you can produce a sharply outlined circle. You can then buff this wax-gilt circle to a gloss and burnish it to a still higher sheen. However, if you wish, you can leave the gold in its original mat appearance. In either case, such applications should be protected with the acrylic medium. The remaining surfaces finished in acrylic colors can be rendered glossy by means of acrylic medium and finally waxed. (As mentioned, the spraying of large surfaces with an aerosol can is impractical.)

Step-by-Step Refinishing of a Side Table

The mainstays of the techniques employed in refinishing the remaining pieces of furniture are templets and masking tape. The use of these materials requires no particular manual skills. The real secret of success in your refinishing projects is your choice of suitable colors and designs.

The materials used to finish this table are: black, white, burnt siena, and yellow acrylic colors; gold and silver enamel sprays; a compass; a black marker; cheesecloth; a ruler; and masking tape. The raw, unfinished table is seen on page 91. The completely refinished table is seen in color on page 61. A pale yellow acrylic is used as a foundation paint. A description of the procedure used in refinishing the table follows (see diagram, page 91).

Step 1. Spray surface A with black enamel after protecting the rest of the table top with paper and masking tape. Follow this quickly with gold enamel. Spray it sparingly onto the black surface, so as not to obliterate the black underneath.

Step 2. When the enameled surface is dry, wet it with soapy water. Spray silver enamel lightly over the enameled surface and texture it with wet absorbent paper.

Step 3. Protect the now black, gold, and silver surface A. Apply burnt siena acrylic color thinned with water to surface D. Texture the acrylic with cheesecloth.

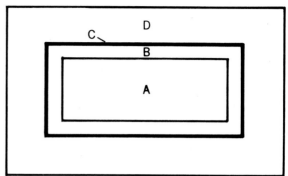

Side Table, Before Refinishing. Here is the table in its original condition with all its old paint removed.

Side Table, Diagram for Top. The various areas of the design have been painted in the following colors: (A) gold and silver spray enamels on a black enamel foundation; (B) gold spray enamel border; (C) black marker; and (D) burnt siena acrylic glaze textured with a sponge.

Side Table, Refinished. Here is the table completely refinished according to the diagram shown above. See page 61 for a color view of the table's top.

Step 4. With black marker draw border C ¼″ or ½″ from enameled surface. Protect surface D (the one textured with burnt siena together with black border C) and surface A with masking tape and paper (the latter used for the large surfaces). Spray gold enamel on the remaining ¼″ (or ½″) to produce border B.

Step 5. Mark the curved lines in the corners of the black border with a compass (equipped with the nylon-tipped marker), and fill the corners with black marker.

Step 6. Paint the knob of the drawer and the legs with black acrylic. An identical method is used to finish the face of the drawer, but because the drawer is so narrow, the gold border is omitted.

The top of the table as well as its drawer should be perfectly smooth. When using an acrylic paint to cover its knob and legs, take care to thin the paint sufficiently and thus avoid brushmarks that will leave a prominent texture. In painting the legs and the drawer knob, the underlying yellow foundation can be utilized. Hence, instead of the black acrylic paint, you could use a light spray of black enamel, thus allowing the black and yellow colors to interchange. The effect of this procedure produces an extraordinarily effective finish which can be applied on some areas of the furniture discussed on the following pages.

Step-by-Step Refinishing of a Small Bench

The original condition of this bench can be seen on page 93. The materials needed to refinish it are: yellow and green acrylic colors; yellow and black spray enamels; masking tape; templets; string; and nails. After the bench has been given a foundation coat of yellow acrylic, the refinishing proceeds as follows (see diagram, page 93):

Step 1. Using a pencil and ruler, divide the bench's top into symmetrical triangles. Cut templets to fit surfaces A and B.

Step 2. With the appropriate templets protect triangles B which still carry the original yellow color and spray black enamel over open triangles A.

Step 3. On both sides of the top of the bench place as many nails as you wish at identical distances from each other. Use the nails as guideposts and attach pieces of string firmly from a nail on one side to its counterpart on the other side along equidistant parallel lines. The holes left after the nails are removed should be filled with acrylic modeling paste.

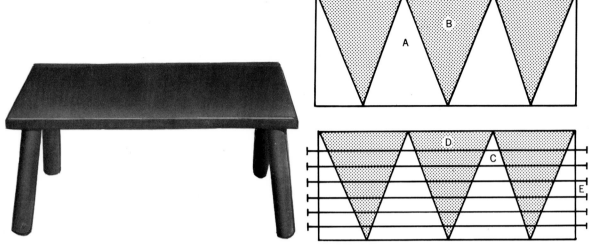

Small Bench, Before Refinishing. After all its old paint has been removed, as shown here, this bench receives an overall coat of light yellow acrylic.

Small Bench, Diagram for Top. The various areas of the design have been painted in the following colors: (A) yellow acrylic foundation color; (B) black spray enamel; (C) black stripes; (D) yellow stripes; and (E) nails and string.

Small Bench, Refinished. Here is the bench refinished according to the diagram seen above. See page 61 for a color view of the bench's top.

Step 4. Protect triangles B with paper templets C. Spray triangles A with yellow enamel, spraying directly on top of the strings. Black lines will be left on the triangles where the strings have protected the underlying surface.

Step 5. Protect triangles A by slipping the templets under the course of strings. Now spray triangles B with black. Protected by the strings, yellow lines will appear, because of the original color of the triangles B.

Step 6. Using either chromium oxide green or a mixture of black (or umber, or phthalo blue) and cadmium yellow acrylic, paint the legs of the table.

The method described may seem complicated, but the technical operations involved are really simple and you can produce an infinite number of pattern and color combinations with them. For example, instead of triangles, you could use circles; the strings could be placed bilaterally, or masking tape of various widths could be attached to the surface to form multicolored rectangles or squares in symmetrical patterns.

Very interesting effects can be achieved by strewing coarse sand at random on a very light surface. Then, spray this surface lightly with a dark color. Next, brush off the sand and apply fresh sand and spray it with another color. Three or four such consecutive applications will result in intriguing patterns of color and texture.

Step-by-Step Refinishing of a Chest

The original condition of the chest is seen on page 95. The materials needed are: yellow oxide, burnt siena, phthalo blue, and white acrylic gesso; masking tape, paper towels, a rubber comb; and a black nylon-tipped marker. A combination of yellow oxide acrylic and white acrylic gesso is used as a foundation color for the piece. The refinishing proceeds as follows (see diagram, page 95):

Step 1. Outline the pattern with a pencil on the front of the chest, and isolate surfaces B and C with masking tape.

Step 2. Apply a burnt siena glaze to surface A and texture the glaze with a rubber comb. (Each of the four segments of this area should be combed separately.)

Step 3. Uncover surfaces B and C and place masking tape around the

Chest, Before Refinishing. Here is the chest in its untreated condition. A combination of yellow oxide acrylic and white acrylic gesso is used as a foundation color over the entire piece.

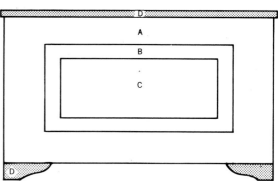

Chest, Diagram for Front. The various areas of the design have been painted in the following colors: (A) burnt siena glaze textured with a rubber comb over a light yellow acrylic foundation; (B) original yellow color of the foundation coat; (C) phthalo blue glaze textured with crumpled, dry paper towel; and (D) solid phthalo blue acrylic.

Chest, Refinished Front. Refinished according to the diagram shown above, this chest can be seen in color on page 61.

outside edges of surface C. Next glaze surface C with phthalo blue, and texture the glaze with a crumpled (dry) piece of paper towel.

Step 4. Outline all the color fields with the black nylon-tipped marker and paint the base D and the top molding D of the chest with phthalo blue acrylic. The sides of the chest should be finished in a burnt siena glaze, and combed horizontally in order to continue the striations that appear on the face of the chest. The top should be a solid phthalo blue.

The decoration of the chest proceeds along the lines of the Tyrolian peasant style—a style that was popular during the early part of the eighteenth century. As a matter of fact, the idea for this finish was derived from an object preserved in the Volksart Museum in Innsbruck, Austria.

The original "antique" finish was executed on a gesso foundation (the traditional gesso employed glue as its binder) with colors that were generally compounded with oil (linseed oil); the surface appearance of such a finish is always mat. Although originally the surface might have been varnished and therefore glossy, that antique chest had acquired a mat surface. Hence, as a final finish, I suggest using the acrylic mat varnish. These varnishes differ with various manufacturers. Therefore, I recommend a brand with which I am familiar; it is produced by Permanent Pigments and carries the brand name Liquitex.

Step-by-Step Refinishing of a Door

The original condition of the door before refinishing can be seen on page 97. The materials needed to refinish this door are: phthalo blue and red oxide acrylic colors, gold spray enamel, paper, masking tape, a pencil, and a ruler. After the door has been given a foundation coat of phthalo blue acrylic, the refinishing proceeds as follows (see diagram, page 97):

Step 1. Spray the entire B and C areas of the panels lightly with gray enamel. Of course, the rest of the door's adjoining surfaces must be protected, using paper and masking tape. When panels B and C are dry, divide them into segments, using a pencil and a ruler.

Step 2. Place masking tape around the borders of segments C and paint them with red oxide acrylic.

Step 3. Place masking tape alongside all the moldings of the inside panels and protect the rest of the adjoining surfaces with paper. Next, spray moldings D with gold enamel.

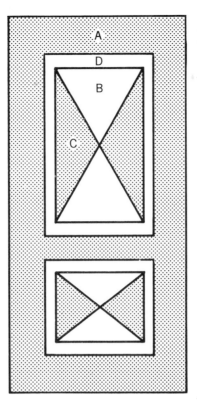

Door, Before Refinishing. Here is the door in its original condition with most of its old paint, as well as its knob, removed.

Door, Diagram for Front. The various areas of the design have been painted in the following colors: (A) foundation coat of phthalo blue acrylic; (B) light gray spray enamel; (C) red oxide acrylic; and (D) gold spray enamel border.

Door, Refinished. Here is the front of the door refinished according to the diagram. See page 62 for a color view of the door.

The size of a normally proportioned door makes the use of acrylic paint preferable for priming large surfaces. But to achieve certain interchanging color effects such as those seen on surface B in the diagram of the door, spray enamel must be used.

In this example there are only two panels in the door, and these are of different sizes. However, no matter how many panels a door may have, the decoration within each panel should remain the same. As a general rule, the colors should be limited to two, or three at the most, in order to avoid creating stark, restless patterns. If you wish, panels B and C can be decorated with the delicate simulation of marble. For the final finish on the door, you should use a mat varnish.

Step-by-Step Refinishing of a Highboy

The highboy can be seen in its original condition on page 99. The materials which you will need to refinish this piece are: burnt siena, yellow oxide, and black acrylic colors; masking tape; a compass; paper towels; a ruler; and a felt-tipped marker. Burnt siena acrylic is used as the foundation coat for this highboy. The procedure for refinishing this piece is as follows (see diagram, page 99):

Step 1. When the burnt siena foundation has dried, mix yellow oxide acrylic with white acrylic gesso and cover front A of each drawer. Then, glaze this yellow with burnt siena acrylic. While it is still wet, texture the glaze with a crumpled (dry) piece of paper towel. (See Chapter 3 for the specific glazing technique.)

Step 2. With a marker, draw black outline B around each of the drawers. Mark off the rounding of the corners with a compass and fill these segments in with black acrylic.

Step 3. Paint area C as well as the sides of the highboy with solid burnt siena acrylic.

Step 4. Paint base D and top molding D of the highboy with black acrylic. The sides of the highboy should be finished in solid burnt siena acrylic.

To look well, all the surfaces of the highboy should be perfectly smooth. Therefore, as usual, several thin layers of acrylic paint will have to be applied. When dry, use fine steel wool in parallel, horizontal strokes to provide a mirror-like finish. However, because of their thinness and, therefore, vulnerability, don't rub the glazed parts with steel wool.

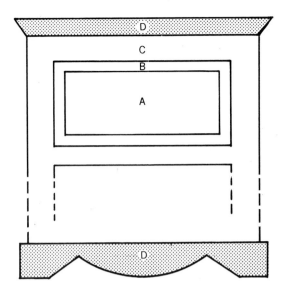

Highboy, Diagram for Front. (Left) The various areas of the design have been painted in the following colors: (A) burnt siena glaze textured with crumpled paper towel over a yellow oxide acrylic foundation; (B) black marker; (C) solid burnt siena acrylic; and (D) black acrylic.

Highboy, Before Refinishing. (Below, Left) Notice that on the bottom half of the highboy the burnt siena acrylic foundation coat has been applied; the top remains in a "raw" condition.

Highboy, Refinished. (Below) Here is the front of the highboy refinished according to the diagram shown above. See page 62 for a color view of the highboy.

Finally, wax and polish the highboy to a high gloss; this suggests a "hand rubbed" finish. Another method of producing a perfectly smooth surface on the acrylic paint is to douse the paint liberally with water using a flat squirrel-hair brush. This must be done at the moment just before the paint solidifies completely, and thus becomes unmovable. To be successful, such an operation requires perfect timing.

Step-by-Step Refinishing of a Chair

The materials required to refinish this chair include: black and white acrylic paints, gold spray enamel, varnish, masking tape, a sponge, and a brush. The refinishing proceeds as described in the following:

Step 1. After sandpapering the raw wood thoroughly, paint the entire chair with black acrylic.

Step 2. Spray gold enamel on the rail and parts of the rods and legs designated A as illustrated on page 101. There is no need to protect the parts that are to remain black, designated B.

Step 3. Now apply masking tape over the gold next to the areas that are to be finished in black, and repaint these parts with black. By using masking tape, a sharp division between gold and black can easily be established.

Step 4. Thinly cover a sheet of soft paper (a few inches larger than the chair's seat) with white acrylic paint diluted with water.

Step 5. Apply a glaze of black acrylic to seat C. While the seat is still wet, press the sheet of paper that has been covered with the white acrylic onto the glazed area.

Step 6. Remove the paper quickly and retouch the texture where needed with a sponge.

Step 7. Now remove the masking tape and protect only the finish of the seat with a semigloss varnish.

The decoration of the chair differs stylistically from the rest of the objects in this chapter inasmuch as it echoes some characteristics of furniture from the period of the *Empire* (corresponding with the English Regency Style) during the early nineteenth century.

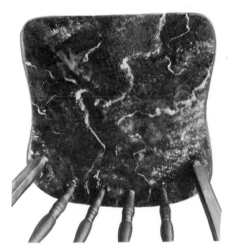

Chair, Back and Legs. The areas designated A are finished with gold spray enamel. Those marked B are painted with black acrylic.

Chair, Seat. The seat of the chair is marbled with a combination of black and white acrylic. Soft paper is used to apply the white acrylic to the still wet black acrylic of the seat. The entire chair and seat can be seen in color on page 63.

Correcting Mistakes

The procedures described on the preceding pages are simple, requiring no special ingenuity or skill. Yet, a perfect result may not be achieved by someone totally inexperienced in handling a ruler, a compass, or masking tape. Therefore, minor errors may occur; a line may not be perfectly straight, or some spots may require repainting, and so on.

For example, the kind of straight edge you may like to see on the dark borders dividing the various fields of color could appear ragged after the removal of your masking tape. But your nylon-tipped marker and a ruler will take care of such imperfections provided, of course, that these borders are sufficiently dark—as they will be on almost every occasion.

The various colored fields (endowed with particular textures made with sponges, cheesecloth, or any other conceivable tools) are usually created with glazes. To make any correction in such glazes, the original underlying color ("the foundation") should first be applied to cover up the spot that needs correction. Then, the appropriate glazing and texturing can be carried out.

6

Finishing Frames

The first frames I shall discuss are made of several simple moldings. The first type of molding is called "back band" (Figure 21) and the second type is called "cove" (Figure 22). Both are standard lumberyard moldings. Ready-made, unfinished frames of oak or chestnut in simple designs can be obtained from art supply stores, and the appropriate finishes for these will also be discussed here. Moldings of your own design can be ordered from lumberyards. All frames, except those exceeding 25" x 30", will be enhanced when used with an insert, which is described on page 108.

The following finishes on appropriate frames will be discussed: metallic effects (gold and silver) on narrow moldings, colored effects on wider moldings, natural wood finishes and combed effects on ready-made frames, and a combination of several treatments.

Let's start with the narrow back band or cove moldings; they can be used to frame all kinds of pictures: oils, watercolors, drawings, and prints. However, these moldings will require inserts, or cardboard mats, depending on the nature of the pictures. For oil paintings, wood inserts from 1½" to 3" wide will be needed. Prints and watercolors look best when matted.

Gold Enamel Finish

Although the molding (you can use either back band or cove) is, as a rule, quite smooth, it should first be treated with fine steel wool before applying the metallic finish. The metallic paints should be sprayed from a distance of about 10" using short "dusting" strokes. Do not allow the paint to pile up. Therefore, make your first application of enamel, as well as the subsequent ones, quite thin. When the foundation spray is dry, it

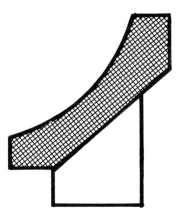

Figure 21. This narrow type of molding is called "back band" molding (available in lumberyards) and looks well when gilded or sprayed with gold enamel.

Figure 22. This narrow molding also used for frames is called "cove" molding (available in lumberyards).

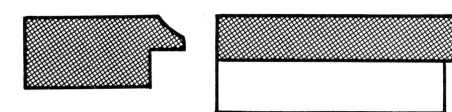

Figure 23. Here are two different sizes of inserts: the insert on the left has a one inch width; the insert on the right has a two inch width. Inserts can be covered with linen or with acrylic gesso.

could also be made perfectly smooth with very fine steel wool. Gold and silver applications can be used interchangeably. The required materials are gold and/or silver spray enamels, umber acrylic paint, a burnisher, steel wool, and cheesecloth. The step-by-step procedure follows:

Step 1. Spray the molding with gold or silver enamel; this will serve as a foundation coat.

Step 2. When the enamel has dried, smooth its surface with very fine steel wool.

Step 3. Spray the molding again with gold or silver spray.

Step 4. When the paint has dried thoroughly, burnish its surface.

Step 5 (optional). If you want an antique effect, cover the metallic enamel with a burnt umber acrylic glaze.

Step 6. Burnish the surface again, and protect it with clear plastic spray. Burnishing should proceed when the sprayed surface becomes perfectly hard. Depending on the brand of the enamel and the thickness of the application, this may take from 2 to 20 hours. Should you wish to antique the metallic finish, do so before burnishing, because a smooth, glossy surface does not readily accept an acrylic glaze. The glaze will always turn mat when it drys. Therefore, a subsequent burnishing will be necessary. For the final protection of the finish, you can use clear plastic spray.

Wax Gilding of Frames

Another way to produce a metallic finish on frames (in this case, still those made of narrow moldings) is to use wax gilt. However, the metallic spray enamels are preferable because they produce a harder surface. The step-by-step procedure for using wax gilt follows:

Step 1. Make the surface of the molding nonabsorbent by covering it with acrylic medium. Next, rub the surface with very fine steel wool and seal the surface once again. (Enamel spray can be also used for sealing.)

Step 2. Rub the wax-gilt paste into the surface with your finger or with a piece of cheesecloth. With a soft cloth polish the gilt to a high gloss.

Step 3. After at least 24 hours, burnish the surface. This burnishing will produce a cohesive metallic surface of high gloss.

Step 4 (optional). If you want an antique effect, cover the gilt surface with a burnt umber acrylic glaze and texture the glaze with cheesecloth.

Step 5. When the wax gilt is dry, rub the acrylic medium thinly into this finish. This is best done with your finger; you can also use a clear plastic spray.

It bears repeating that burnishing should be done on a wax surface that has become sufficiently solidified. Therefore, a waiting period of at least 24 hours is recommended. It should also proceed without undue pressure. Wax gilding is very simple, very effective, and permanent; it will not tarnish. But because it is not as hard as the spray enamel, it should be protected either with acrylic medium or with clear plastic spray.

Sometimes it is quite effective to have certain profiles (ridges or raised areas) of a molding polished to high luster. They provide a contrast to their adjoining, perfectly flat, gilded surfaces. Such effects are not uncommon on antique objects. To produce a mat surface, all you have to do is to apply the wax gilt without buffing it. However, such a flat finish is vulnerable. Therefore, after allowing the gilt to harden during a period of about a week, protect it with the acrylic medium.

An Alternate Gilding Method

Gold leaf comes in 3⅜″ squares; when trying to simulate the effect of gold leaf, you can use the following procedure. Place a stiff paper with a good hard edge on your molding. Apply the wax-gilt paste over the paper's edge for a distance of about 2″. Then, place the paper at a distance of 3⅜″ (from the starting point). In this instance, proceed with the gilding in the reverse direction, thus covering all of the 3⅜″. The next section should be applied closely to the first so as to suggest the presence of another gold leaf. Allow just the width of a hair between them.

Colored Burlwood Finish

Narrow moldings such as the back band, cove, or differently profiled moldings not exceeding a 1½″ width can receive a finish that simulates the effects of burlwood seen in the color plate on page 53. The materials required to produce this finish are: yellow spray enamel, burnt umber acrylic, cheesecloth, steel wool, and acrylic medium or clear plastic spray. The step-by-step procedure follows:

Step 1. Make sure your molding has a very smooth surface. Spray it with yellow enamel.

Step 2. Polish the enameled surface with very fine steel wool and spray it again.

Step 3. When the enamel is dry, remove its gloss with the steel wool; glaze the enamel with burnt umber acrylic. While the acrylic is still wet, texture it with cheesecloth.

Step 4. Rub acrylic medium into the dry, glazed surface to produce a high gloss, or spray it with clear plastic spray.

The opaque burlwood finish described above seems to be the only colored finish appropriate for narrow moldings. Transparent finishes that allow the grain of the wood to show are effective only on oak or chestnut moldings, that is, on a richly grained wood.

Another Antique Finish

You may have some of the "old fashioned" Barbizon type frames that, originally gilded, have by now lost their luster. To refinish them you may simply spray them with gold enamel, but too much gold results in a certain gaudiness. Hence, an "antique" finish on such frames will considerably improve their looks. The step-by-step procedure will be as follows:

Step 1. Replace any missing parts of the frame's ornaments with the acrylic modeling paste.

Step 2. Upon drying, spray the entire frame with red enamel color, and allow it to harden completely.

Step 3. Spray the frame with gold enamel. When the enamel is dry, remove the gold from the top of the ornaments with very fine steel wool.

Step 4. Brush soapy water over the surface, working it vigorously into all interstices. This is done to allow the subsequent application of the patina (white acrylic gesso and umber acrylic) to go over the enameled surface without trickling. While still wet, wipe the gray patina from the molding; it will only remain in the interstices of the ornaments.

This finish will give the frame a faded "antique" appearance. Buffing or waxing the surface is not recommended.

Suiting Your Frame to Your Picture

What kind of pictures would look best when framed in the back band molding, or any molding not exceeding 1½″? (As mentioned, a mat or an insert should always be used when such moldings are chosen.) Black and white work (etchings, lithographs, woodcuts, prints) should be framed only in black or metallic moldings (gold or silver). Frames with a burlwood finish should be used on oil paintings not exceeding the size of about 12″ x 16″. In other words, larger oil paintings will require wider moldings.

The Linen-Covered Insert

The term insert refers to an intermediate, flat frame that separates the picture from its frame proper (Figure 23). It is made always of wood ranging in width from at least 1″ to not more than 2½″; in contrast the *mat* is made of cardboard or cardboard-covered fabric and its width should be, as a rule, 2″ to 3″.

There are two principal types of coverings for inserts: raw linen or acrylic gesso. Linen suitable for this purpose (essentially the same used by artists for painting with oils) should possess a fine, regular texture. For very small paintings (about 10″ x 12″) bleached linen, or even silk, can be used. The fabric should be attached to the surface of the wood insert in the following manner:

Step 1. Cut the linen to a size one inch larger all around than the size of the insert.

Step 2. Cover the wood surface of the insert generously with white synthetic glue. Allow the glue to thicken, or else it will penetrate to the reverse side of the linen.

Step 3. Place the linen on the insert and press it down—*but let the linen surface sag considerably over the opening of the frame called, the "window."* This is done by simply pressing down vigorously on the linen lying over the window. The purpose of this operation is to secure enough of the material for pulling it over the inner edge of the insert and attaching it into the rabbet (the slot or joint where two strips of wood or molding meet).

Step 4. Turn the canvas-covered insert face down, and with a razor blade cut out the linen over the window. At the same time cut the linen into the rabbet of the molding. Allow 1″ of the material to serve for attachment over the edge.

Step 5. Now cover this inch of the canvas, as well as the rabbet, with the white glue; use a small, stiff-bristle brush for this purpose.

Step 6. Next, cut the 1″ strip diagonally to all corners to allow the linen to be folded into the corner of the rabbet.

The Gesso-Covered Insert

Instead of linen, an insert can have an acrylic gesso covering. The acrylic gesso used for this purpose should be thinned with water to avoid leaving brushstrokes on its surface. When the white gesso is dry, a gray patina can be spread thinly on it. The reason for using the patina is to provide a wider insert with a more varied color effect. If the width of the insert does not exceed about 1″, its color could be white or a light gray of uniform tonality. If you want such a light gray, mix the white gesso with raw or burnt umber acrylic. Cooler tonality will result if some blue is added to the umber-gesso mixture.

You may ask whether any other color scheme could be chosen for this purpose. Theoretically, of course, any combination of colors could be used, but for all practical purposes a *neutral* gray color will do best, because it will not interfere with any existing color scheme in the painting. The gesso finish of the insert should always be mat. A glossy appearance on such a surface would be quite disturbing.

The required materials for producing a gessoed insert are: acrylic white gesso, umber and phthalo blue acrylics, and a utility brush.

Step 1. Mix thinned acrylic gesso with your chosen colors and brush the mixture on the wooden insert. Avoid producing visible brushstrokes.

Step 2. Sandpaper the gessoed surface lightly and apply a second, thinner coat of the same color.

Patining of the Insert

If an insert is wider than 1″, in certain instances variations of the over-all gray tone may be desirable. Such muted tonal effects can be produced by application of a lighter patina on top of a darker foundation. The procedure follows:

Step 1. Cover the wooden insert with a gray acrylic gesso. This is a combination of white acrylic gesso and umber acrylic. Should a cooler tone be more appropriate for the occasion, you can add some phthalo blue acrylic.

Step 2. Prepare a gesso of a much thinner consistency, considerably lighter in color; brush this "patina" all over the insert.

Step 3. Now rub the patina gently with very fine steel wool.

Durability of Inserts

The linen-covered insert is, as a rule, more desirable. However, such an insert, especially when made of a smooth and light linen, is quite vulnerable. An excess of the liquid adhesive used for its attachment, as well as other hazards, may stain it. Should this happen, even in a very small spot, the entire surface will require refinishing. Also, linen may become detached here and there forming ungainly blisters. Such emergencies will call for the vigorous brushing of white synthetic glue (thinned a little with water). This brushing will force the adhesive to penetrate the fabric and thus affect its reattachment. However, this operation will slightly alter the linen's color; therefore it will have to be carried out over the entire surface of the linen.

When stained, a thin gray gesso brushed over the entire linen insert will equalize its color without radically altering the texture of the fabric.

Finishing Hardwood Frames

Ready-made oak and chestnut frames (Figures 24 and 25) are available in standard sizes (10" x 12", 12" x 16", 16" x 20", 20" x 24", and so on) in most of the larger art supply stores. The only finish that seems to suit these wood frames is patination. The required materials are umber acrylic and white acrylic gesso. The procedure follows:

Step 1. Darken the color of the oak or chestnut frame with raw or burnt umber acrylic (the second is warmer and darker in tone).

Step 2. Prepare the patina by combining white acrylic gesso and umber acrylic thinned considerably with water. When the underlying coat of umber acrylic has dried, brush the patina onto the frame. The patina should be much lighter in color than the umber-covered surface of the

Figure 24. This ready-made chestnut frame has been finished with a gray patina produced from white acrylic gesso and umber acrylic.

Figure 25. This ready-made oak frame has also received the gray patina which is the only finish that seems to suit it.

frame. While the patina is still wet, rub the excess off with a moist rag. This allows the patina to remain imbedded in the grain of the wood.

Step 3. Rub the patina-covered surface with steel wool to produce a faint sheen.

Frames with Textured Finishes

Wooden frames composed of wider moldings can be finished with a combed pattern. This pattern is produced with acrylic modeling paste thinned to an appropriate consistency and then textured with a rubber comb (Figures 26 and 27). The acrylic paste can be tinted either with umber or phthalo blue thinned to the consistency of watercolor. A dense gray patina can also be used on these wider frames. In both instances sandpapering of their surfaces will produce the final textural and coloristic effect (Figures 28 and 29).

The required materials are: white acrylic gesso, acrylic modeling paste, umber and phthalo blue acrylic, a utility brush about 2″ wide, a rubber comb (or hair comb), and medium coarse as well as fine sandpaper. The procedure follows:

Step 1. Without diluting it, brush the gesso over the entire frame and allow the gesso to dry.

Step 2. Place some of the modeling paste in a saucer and add a little water to make it brushable. Apply the paste with the utility brush.

Step 3. Run your comb through the paste to produce the textures you want. Let the paste dry thoroughly.

Step 4. Next, sandpaper the rough surface.

Step 5. Thin the umber and phthalo blue acrylic to "watercolor" consistency. Brush the colors over the entire frame—the ridges as well as the grooves.

Step 6. Sandpaper the finish to produce the proper blending of color and surface texture.

Texturing with Comb and Acrylic Paste

Because of the rapid drying of acrylic modeling paste, it is advisable to make your surface nonabsorbent before you apply it. Although your

Figure 26. Wooden frames composed of wider moldings can be finished with a texture produced from acrylic modeling paste and patterned with a rubber comb.

Figure 27. The rubber comb can produce an infinite variety of patterns in the acrylic modeling paste such as the curved one shown here.

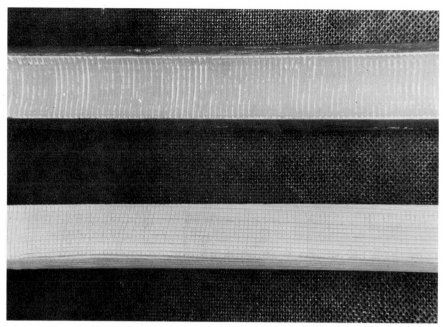

Figure 28. Here are two more examples of patterns that can be produced with a rubber comb and acrylic modeling paste.

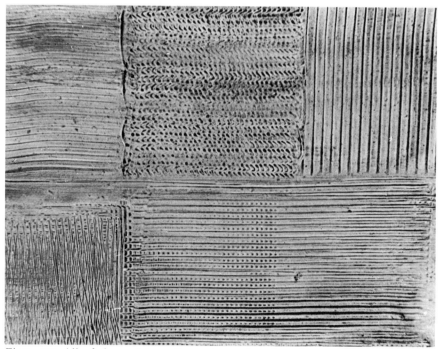

Figure 29. All of the various patterns shown here have been achieved by "combing" a shallow layer of acrylic modeling paste which is then glazed with a darker color.

initial coat of the acrylic gesso is largely nonabsorbent, brushing some of the acrylic medium on it will increase this condition. The consistency of the modeling paste is also important. When it is too thin, you will not be able to texture it with a comb because the layer of the paste will not retain the marks of the comb's teeth. When the paste is too dense, combing will prove to be difficult. You must also maintain the proper thickness of the paste application so that the marks of the comb are neither too shallow nor too deep.

For successful combing the consistency of the paste, once it covers the frame, must be just right. Therefore, allow the paste to settle, that is to lose some of its liquid quality, before you run the comb through it. Because the paste dries quickly, do not try to work at one time on more than 30″ of the frame's length. Also remember that although the top surface of the paste may appear solidified, it will remain soft inside for a much longer time. Therefore, before sandpapering the paste, make sure that it has hardened throughout.

Coloring Acrylic Paste

Now a word about the coloring of the white acrylic modeling paste. I have suggested umber and phthalo blue acrylic for use on frames with a textured finish. When these two colors are mixed together, a blue-black or brown-black color will result, depending on the preponderance of one or the other color. But, because you apply this colored paste very thinly (that is, in the consistency of watercolor), on the white gesso surface, it will appear gray. A solid gray may not always be desirable. To vary it, you may brush on the brown and the blue colors separately but in close proximity to each other, not necessarily as an intimate mixture.

Final sandpapering in this procedure has a dual function: by removing the coloring from the ridges of the combed surface some of the original white gesso color will register in tiny spots. Together with the colors imbedded in the rough texture and the grooves of the combed texture, the surface will acquire a faded, "antique" appearance.

Should you desire any change in color, subsequent applications of the thinned paint can be made, followed always by sandpapering. A high gloss on such surfaces does not look well, hence waxing or varnishing of these textured frames is inadvisable.

The question now arises whether any color other than gray could be used for the coloring of the molding. Theoretically, of course, any color could be chosen—as long as it appears neutral, that is, bleached out to a point where it will not clash with the colors used in the painting. According to general experience, however, a muted gray of a warm or cool tonality will be suitable for all occasions, no matter what colors may predominate in a given painting.

Gilding the Profiles of Frames

The narrow *profiles* of a frame composed of wide (5″ or more) moldings which have been textured are usually found at the outside and/or inside borders of the molding. These profiles can be either flat or carved (Figure 30) and look attractive when they are gilded. The required materials are: wax gilt and a burnisher.

Gilding by means of the wax-gold compound is described on page 67. The only precaution to be taken before gilding of such profiles, or subsidiary areas of a frame, is to provide a perfectly smooth surface for them. Remember that the molding that forms the frame has been painted with gesso before the modeling paste used for texturing is applied. As soon as the gesso solidifies superficially, the profiles that are to be gilded should be rubbed with fine abrasive paper. To repeat, it is not easy to remove the brushmarks in a well-hardened acrylic gesso, although when such surfaces are moistened this task becomes less difficult. Take care not to let the modeling paste used for combing get on the profiles. Once these profiles are perfectly smooth, you can proceed to apply wax gilt directly on their white gessoed surface. Burnishing of the gilt should be done after it attains a certain degree of hardness; therefore, a waiting time of at least 24 hours is recommended. If you want to "antique" the gilding, use burnt umber acrylic. Texture the umber glaze with cheesecloth and finally burnish the glaze to achieve the right luster.

Restoring the Carved Details of a Frame

Modeling paste can be used to restore missing parts of ornaments carved in the wood of a frame or those made of a composition material. In its original condition, acrylic modeling paste can not be shaped with your fingers (like modeling clay, for example); it will also not respond readily to the action of a stylus or a modeling tool (Figure 31). However, when the paste is mixed with an extra fine sawdust (or, still better, with bronze or aluminum powder), it becomes much easier to shape—even with your fingers—because it takes on a much denser consistency.

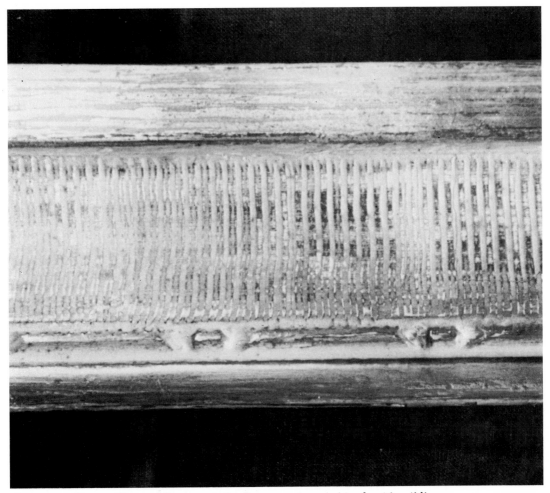

Figure 30. On a wider molding combed effects can be combined with gilding. Inner and outer profiles can be gilded with the wax-gold compound.

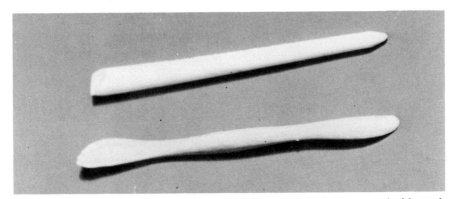

Figure 31. The stylus (above) and the modeling tool (below) are valuable tools for repairing the carved details of old frames. They are used in conjunction with a mixture composed of acrylic modeling paste and either sawdust or bronze powder.

Figure 32. Acrylic modeling paste can be used to repair cracks, such as the one seen in the upper right-hand corner. It can also be used to replace broken or missing details that have been carved into the wood of a frame.

Before joining the new part, composed of the acrylic paste and sawdust, to the frame, the surfaces of attachment should be moistened with acrylic medium. If the part to be attached is too big, the acrylic medium may prove to be too weak an adhesive. In such instances, remove the newly constructed, semi-dry part; allow the part to dry well. Then attach it again with white synthetic glue or epoxy glue.

Acrylic modeling paste that has been mixed with sawdust dries more slowly than it does in its original condition.

7

Repairing Stone and Refinishing Metal

In my book, *Restoring and Preserving Antiques,* I described many methods for producing patinas on a variety of metals such as silver, pewter, iron, copper, bronze, and brass. These patinas ranged from light oxidations to encrustations commonly found on objects of great antiquity. In this book, however, because I am addressing the novice, I shall limit myself to the most simple procedures for producing patinas on objects made of copper and its alloys, bronze and brass.

Patinas on Copper and Brass

Why condition in any manner the glistening surfaces of copper, bronze, or brass? It all depends on the nature of the metal object and its uses. A highly polished, glistening surface may be desirable for one item, but on another item just the opposite condition—a heavy oxidation and patination suggesting antiquity—may be mandatory.

In the color plate on page 64 the two small decorative vases on the far left and right respectively are made of copper. On these items even an archeological incrustation would be, by far, more interesting than a well-groomed polish, which could in no way enhance their decorative appeal. If you prefer the brass candlestick holder in the center—an item quite common before and during the gaslight era—in a shiny condition, well and good. But if the brassy sheen should ruffle your sensibilities, you may wish to produce a vitreous blue-green patina on its surface as shown on page 64.

The patinas to be discussed can be accomplished with the simplest materials; the handling of them should present no difficulty, even to a novice. The required materials for the following two patinas are: a common kitchen variety of salt and vinegar; iron (ferric) chloride which is a noncorrosive acid salt used in etching copper plates and available in chemical supply stores; and liver of sulphur (potassium polysulphide) which is a common noncorrosive chemical obtainable in drug stores. Both chemicals are harmless and will not irritate either your skin or lungs (if inhaled).

Preliminary Rubbing and Oxidation

As mentioned, a glossy well-polished surface of copper, brass, or bronze will not readily take on a patina. Therefore, it is necessary to remove the original sheen of these metals. Roughing up the surface, as well as the oxidation of it, facilitate this patina process, and promote a better attachment. Moreover, when treating bronze or brass objects of different manufacture (because their alloys are, more likely than not, differently proportioned), you cannot expect an identical response to the treatment.

By rubbing with fine steel wool you can remove the sheen from a metal object. Next, the surface of the metal must be oxidized. There are two methods of oxidation: one is natural, and the other is man-made. Oxidation is produced naturally by exposing metal to the elements; however this process is quite slow. A faster method is to cover a piece of metal with a solution of liver of sulphur that has reached the point of saturation. (When a residue has formed in the bottom of the container holding the solution, you know that saturation has taken place.) When oxidizing metal, you should stop the process before the metal turns black.

Producing a Blue-Green Patina

When treating a metal object with salt and vinegar, you should understand that salt crystals will form on the metal. Because of the hygroscopic quality of salt, it will attract moisture from the air, thus producing and prolonging the condition of patination. Patination causes the color of the metal to become an intense blue-green of particular beauty. Hence, it stands to reason that even after the desired color has been achieved, exposure to high humidity for many weeks and even months is indicated, for the durability of the patina is contingent upon it. The step-by-step procedure follows:

Step 1. After you have removed the metal's sheen and oxidized its surface, mix up a solution of vinegar and salt. Brush this solution onto the object about six times a day. Continue the procedure for several weeks, that is, until a solid, bluish-green patina covers the metal's surface thoroughly.

Step 2. Allow the metal object to remain in this condition for at least six months. Then, you can eliminate the salt incrustation by washing it off with water.

Step 3. To deepen the resulting color, you can wax the object or coat it with a clear plastic spray.

Producing a Brown-Yellow-Green Patina

When a metal object is exposed to the action of an iron chloride solution, a piece of copper should first be submerged in the solution or, still better, dissolved in it. This makes the solution more reactive. As a matter of fact, when a sufficient amount of copper residue forms in the iron chloride solution, deposit the residue on the object, in order to enhance the color resulting from the patination. The step-by-step procedure follows:

Step 1. Remove the sheen from the metal object and oxidize the metal as described in the procedure on page 123.

Step 2. Saturate a piece of flannel with the iron chloride solution (1:4 in water). Wrap the flannel tightly around the object; allow the cloth to remain wet for several hours.

Step 3. Repeat this treatment until you achieve the desired coloration of the metal.

Protecting Patinas

When you complete the patina procedures, I suggest you spray the object with a coat of clear plastic spray or wax it. (The acrylic medium can be also used for this purpose.) When your patina has been thoroughly established over many months, the change of color produced by wax or plastic spray will be slight. A freshly created patina, however, may darken considerably. Such an effect may, or may not, be desirable, depending upon the particular object. The same can be said of the resulting gloss that wax or a varnish may impart to it. As a rule, a high gloss will be inappropriate; on the other hand, a perfectly mat surface may appear dull. All these cir-

cumstances must be taken into consideration before proceeding with
polishing or waxing.

Combination of Patinas

Should you apply the vinegar-salt combination or merely vinegar or salt
after or before the treatment with iron chloride? How often should
this be done? Here "art" enters, and mechanical manipulation leaves.
These patinas cannot be formulated with the exactness of, say, medicines;
absolute uniformity of effects cannot be achieved very well. What is more
to the point, such uniformity does not appear to be desirable. The charm
and intrigue of a patina lies in the very capriciousness which governs the
appearance of its end-result.

Patina on Modern Pewter

The composition of modern pewter differs from that of "antique" pewter.
Modern pewter lacks the mellowness and characteristic texture of the
antique metal which was used for kitchen utensils. Today, of course,
vessels made of pewter serve merely decorative purposes. It is quite simple
to antique modern pewter. All you have to do is brush diluted sulphuric
acid on the pewter. This acid is the same liquid used for refilling automobile batteries. The length of exposure to the action of the acid will
determine the amount of patina produced.

Repairing Stone Objects

When discussing patinas on copper and its alloys, I was talking about
chemical changes in the body of these metals. When dealing with stone,
however, regardless of its chemical nature, a patina can only be produced
by superficial coloring. The acrylic paints can provide this coloration.

Tinting Coarse Stone

To alter the color of stone with a coarse texture, such as limestone or
cement, all you have to do is to brush on a dry acrylic pigment of the
appropriate color which is well dispersed in water. There is no need to
use the acrylic medium as a binder, because the fine-grained pigment
becomes so firmly imbedded in the pores and minute declivities of the
stone that its removal is practically impossible.

Repairing with Acrylic Paste

Repairs of damaged objects made of such stone as marble, alabaster, and limestone can be made with acrylic modeling paste. The original white color of the paste can be conditioned with an acrylic paint to match the color of the particular stone. For repairing stone with coarse textures, sand may be added to the acrylic paste.

When making repairs, the acrylic paste should be applied in successive layers of about ¼″ thickness. Always leave a jagged surface on the layer to provide better attachment for the following application. (The indicated thickness is suggested in order to prevent fissuring of the paste and to allow it to dry quickly.)

Repairing Terracotta

I assume that an amateur will not venture to replace broken noses or other parts of anatomy or intricate sculpture which would require professional skill. But should you wish to replace a missing or damaged part of a terracotta object, acrylic modeling paste, tinted with an appropriate acrylic color, will serve the purpose well. In its original form, the paste may be too liquid to manage easily. In such a case, allow some of the paste's binder to evaporate before using it. However, be careful; when the paste becomes too stiff, its adhesion to the new surface is impaired.

To improve the paste's adherence to both the surface of the object, as well as the part to be attached, moisten both surfaces with acrylic medium prior to attachment. When the added part hardens sufficiently, a piece of masking tape can be used to hold it in place until the adhesion becomes permanent; this may take up to 24 hours. No further treatment is necessary to harmonize the new piece with the old.

However, if necessary, the tint of the new addition can be easily adjusted to match that of the object with one of the acrylic paints. Although the application of the acrylic paste can be carried out manually, a palette knife and a modeling tool will, on many occasions, prove to be useful for shaping and smoothing the paste.

Repairing Limestone and Marble

Limestone and marble (also alabaster) are closely related in their chemical composition, but they differ in crystalline structure which accounts for the degree of their hardness. Usually, any limestone which possesses colored veins is referred to as "marble." Such stone requires polishing to achieve a high gloss. When repairing limestone or marble, acrylic modeling paste can be used when it is prepared with marble dust and acrylic binder. When this paste mixture is dry and burnished, it will acquire a gloss identical to that of marble or alabaster.

The method of repairing with the paste mixture is the same for both the marble and for the terracotta except for the burnishing. Burnishing can be done either with a steel burnisher (used in etching or polishing copper plates) or, preferably, with the more efficient agate tool. Burnishing should be done by moving the tool swiftly in all directions over the surface of the well-hardened paste, but too much pressure should be avoided.

Repairing and Replacing Large Parts

To provide a proper attachment of a larger piece to the body of a stone object it is advisable to proceed in stages. Build the missing part up gradually, and allow each of the applications of paste to harden completely before proceeding with the next buildup (Figure 33).

When treating objects fashioned of coarse stone, the smooth-textured modeling paste should be mixed with sand so that its texture will match that of the stone. There will never be a difficulty in matching the tint of the stone object, because the acrylic colors are capable of yielding any conceivable nuance. The drying time of the acrylic modeling paste can be substantially shortened by exposing the paste to heat.

Should the texture of the newly-added part be too smooth, roughness can be provided by inflicting marks with a tool, such as an awl, chisel, etc. The step-by-step procedure for repairing limestone with successive buildups of paste follows:

Step 1. Mix the acrylic modeling paste with the acrylic color that matches the stone.

Step 2. Start building up the missing part by applying the paste at a thickness that does not exceed $\frac{1}{4}''$. Leave the newly-created surface jagged.

Step 3. When the first application of paste is dry, continue the buildup in the same manner as above until you reach a point just about $\frac{1}{4}''$ below the level of the original surface.

Step 1. The buildup is started by applying a layer of paste about ¼″ thick.

Step 2. When the first application of paste has dried, the buildup is continued with successive layers until a point is reached just about ¼″ below the level of the original surface.

Figure 33. When repairing a stone object with acrylic modeling paste, the work should proceed in successive stages as shown.

Step 3. The final application of paste is shaped with a palette knife, modeling tool, or stylus to conform with the appearance of the rest of the object.

Figure 34. The marble surface of this antique Corinthian capital became so weathered that it no longer had the glossy appearance of marble. After some repair of the damaged surface, I placed it on a limestone plint. A wash of raw umber acrylic applied to the plint made it conform in color to the color of the capital.

Step 4. Shape the final application with your palette knife or modeling tool to conform with the appearance of the undamaged object. (The procedure described above applies to the replacement of any part which measures from about ½″ upward; shallow damages can be repaired in one operation.)

Repairing Cement

When repairing cement surfaces, a mixture composed of Portland cement with three parts of sand of appropriate fineness (or coarseness, as the case may be) can be used. But instead of mixing these materials with water, acrylic medium should be added to form a workable paste.

In Figure 34 an antique Corinthian capital is seen. Its marble surface became so weathered that the characteristic appearance of its marble was no longer present. I placed the capital on a limestone plint; this limestone came from the San Antonio region of Texas. All I had to do to achieve a perfect homogeneity of the two components was to brush a thin wash of acrylic raw umber dispersed in water onto the plint.

Preservation of Stone Kept Outdoors

It is true that under certain favorable climatic conditions objects made of stone can last "forever." But stone objects, if not fashioned of the hardest stone, will have a relatively short life span when exposed to the rigors of weather. However, weather damage can be minimized if the stone is treated with acrylic medium. The medium penetrates into the minute openings in the stone and creates a membrane which prevents water from settling in these openings. Consequently, erosion is also prevented. Thus, the surface of the stone acquires a protective "skin."

When acrylic medium is thinned with water in the proportion of 1:1, two successive applications with a sturdy brush will prevent the deterioration of stone, even when it is exposed to severe winters. You should allow one or two hours between applications, and repeat the procedure once every few years. The slightly glossy appearance of the acrylic medium will not falisfy the nature of the stone; on the contrary, marble (if not too weathered) will acquire a more marble-like appearance after such a treatment.

Index

Edited by Diane Casella Hines
Designed by James Craig and Robert Fillie
Set in 12 point Garamond by Brown Brothers Linotypers
Printed and bound in Hong Kong by Toppan Printing Company, Ltd.

Cyfrinachau Cyfareddol

a storïau eraill

Emma Thomson

Addasiad Gwenno Mair Davies

Sut i wneud dymuniad gyda Siriol

DYMUNIAD

Mae'r llyfr hwn yn cynnwys dymuniad arbennig iawn i ti
a dy ffrind gorau.

Gyda'ch gilydd, daliwch y llyfr bob pen,
a chau eich llygaid.

Crychwch eich trwynau a meddwl am rif
sy'n llai na deg.

Agorwch eich llygaid, a sibrwd eich rhifau
i glustiau'ch gilydd.

Adiwch y ddau rif gyda'i gilydd. Dyma'ch

Rhif Hud

ti

dy ffrind gorau

Rhowch eich bys bach ar y sêr,
a dweud eich rhif hud yn uchel,
gyda'ch gilydd. Nawr, gwnewch eich dymuniad
yn dawel i'ch hunan. Ac efallai, un diwrnod,
y daw eich dymuniad yn wir.

Cariad mawr

Siriol

x

I Bridget Alice Rani Calthrop
gyda dymuniadau pefriog
E.V.T.

Felicity Wishes © 2000 Emma Thomson
Trwyddedwyd gan White Lion Publishing

Cyhoeddwyd gyntaf ym Mhrydain yn 2005
gan Hodder Children's Books

Cyhoeddwyd gyntaf yn Gymraeg yn 2010 gan
Wasg Gomer, Llandysul, Ceredigion, SA44 4JL.
www.gomer.co.uk

ⓗ testun a'r lluniau: Emma Thomson, 2005 ©
ⓗ testun Cymraeg: Gwenno Mair Davies, 2010 ©

Mae Emma Thomson wedi datgan ei hawl
dan Ddeddf Hawlfreintiau, Dyluniadau a Phatentau 1988
i gael ei chydnabod fel awdur ac arlunydd y llyfr hwn.

ISBN 978 1 84851 133 0

Noddwyd gan Lywodraeth Cynulliad Cymru.

Argraffwyd a rhwymwyd yng Nghymru gan
Wasg Gomer, Llandysul, Ceredigion.

CYNNWYS

Cyfrinachau Cyfareddol

'Mae 'na rywbeth cyfarwydd iawn am y dylwythen deg acw,' sibrydodd Siriol Swyn wrth ei ffrindiau gorau yn ystod y gwasanaeth un bore.

'Oes,' meddai Poli. 'Dwi'n ei hadnabod hi o rywle ond fedra i ddim yn fy myw â chofio o ble.'

'Efallai ein bod ni wedi'i gweld hi yng Nghaffi Seren?' awgrymodd Mali.

'Neu efallai ei bod hi'n enwog,' meddai Moli, gan fynd dros ben llestri braidd. Moli, yn bendant, oedd y dylwythen deg fwyaf dramatig o'r criw.

Roedd Brenhines y Tylwyth Teg ar y llwyfan, yn cyflwyno tylwythen deg swil yr olwg gyda gwallt cyrliog brown, perffaith. Syllodd y ffrindiau arni'n chwilfrydig.

'Dylwyth teg, dyma Ela. Bydd hi'n ymuno â ni yma yn Ysgol y Naw Dymuniad am gyfnod byr i sefyll ei harholiadau terfynol. Rwy'n gobeithio'n fawr y byddwch chi i gyd yn rhoi croeso mawr iddi hi, a'i gwneud yn gartrefol yn ystod ei hamser gyda ni.'

'A dweud y gwir, dwi'n meddwl ei bod hi'n rhywun enwog,' meddai Siriol, gan anghofio sibrwd.

'SIRIOL SWYN!' Taranodd llais Miss Taith ar hyd y neuadd. 'Dim siarad yn ystod y gwasanaeth! Dos i weld y Frenhines ar ôl ysgol am gyfnod cosb.'

Dyna'r pedwerydd tro yr wythnos hon i Siriol gael ei dwrdio am siarad pan nad oedd hi i fod i wneud hynny. Weithiau, roedd hi'n cael ei thynnu i mewn cymaint i sgwrs ddiddorol nes ei bod yn anghofio ble'r oedd hi.

✽ ✽ ✽

Ar ôl yr ysgol safai Siriol
y tu allan i swyddfa
Brenhines y Tylwyth Teg,
gan fyseddu blaen ei ffon
hud yn ddiflas.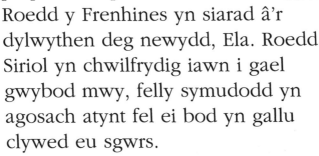

Sylwodd fod drws y
swyddfa'n gilagored, a
phipiodd ei phen i mewn.
Roedd y Frenhines yn siarad â'r
dylwythen deg newydd, Ela. Roedd
Siriol yn chwilfrydig iawn i gael
gwybod mwy, felly symudodd yn
agosach atynt fel ei bod yn gallu
clywed eu sgwrs.

'Rwy'n gwybod nad ydi'r arholiadau
hyn yn hollol angenrheidiol, ond
rydw i wrth fy modd dy fod ti wedi
penderfynu rhoi cynnig arnyn nhw.
Mae'n fraint hefyd i ni dy fod wedi
dewis Ysgol y Naw Dymuniad, a
chofia, os bydd angen unrhyw beth
arnat ti, tyrd i'm gweld i'n syth.'
Ar hynny, agorodd y Frenhines
y drws.

'O, Siriol, do'n i ddim yn gwybod dy fod di yma,' meddai, wedi cynhyrfu'n sydyn.

'Gofynnodd Miss Taith i mi ddod i'ch gweld chi,' meddai Siriol gan frathu'i gwefus. 'Fe ges i fy nal yn siarad yn ystod y gwasanaeth.'

A hithau'n hanner disgwyl cael ei dwrdio, cafodd Siriol ei synnu pan ddywedodd y Frenhines, 'O, paid â phoeni am hynny. Y peth pwysicaf ydi ein bod ni'n gwneud i Ela deimlo'n gartrefol. Fedri di ddangos y ffordd iddi o gwmpas yr ysgol, a gwneud yn siŵr ei bod hi'n setlo'n iawn?'

Doedd hyn yn fawr o gosb i Siriol gan mai hi oedd un o'r tylwyth teg mwyaf cyfeillgar yn Ysgol y Naw Dymuniad. Roedd hi wrth ei bodd yn cael cyfle i wneud ffrindiau newydd.

* * *

Y diwrnod canlynol, hedfanodd Siriol
ac Ela trwy'r dosbarthiadau, yr
ystafelloedd hamdden a'r gerddi hyd
nes bod y ddwy wedi gweld bron pob
twll a chornel o'r ysgol.

Ceisiodd Siriol sgwrsio ag Ela am ei
hysgol ddiwethaf, ond er ei bod hi'n
ymddangos yn gyfeillgar, roedd yn
berffaith amlwg nad oedd Ela am
siarad amdani hi ei hun na'i ffrindiau.
Roedd Siriol wedi'i synnu – pwy
fyddai'n ceisio osgoi siarad am eu
ffrindiau?

Ond roedd gan Ela ddiddordeb
mawr yn ffrindiau Siriol, ac felly buan
iawn yr anghofiodd Siriol am eu sgwrs
ryfedd a dechreuodd rannu hynt a
helynt ei chriw gyda hi. Gallai siarad
am ei ffrindiau am byth.
'. . . a Moli ydi'r
dylwythen deg fwyaf
ffasiynol o'r cyfan,'
byrlymodd Siriol
ar ôl o leiaf

11

hanner awr. 'Hi fydd y Dylwythen Deg brydferthaf a welwyd erioed pan fydd hi wedi graddio.'

Glaniodd Siriol yn flinedig ar fainc yn y ffreutur. 'Dwn i ddim amdanat ti, ond dwi'n llwgu ar ôl yr holl hedfan 'na!'

'A finnau hefyd,' meddai Ela, gan siarad am y tro cyntaf ers hydoedd!

Canodd y gloch amser cinio, ac yn sydyn roedd y ffreutur yn llawn o dylwyth teg llwglyd.

'Helô 'na,' meddai Siriol wrth i Moli, Poli a Mali ymuno â nhw wrth y bwrdd.

'Dyma Ela, mae'n siŵr eich bod chi'n cofio'i gweld yn y gwasanaeth,' meddai Siriol gan ei chyflwyno i bawb.

'Ydw!' meddai Poli yn gyffrous. 'Mae dy wyneb di mor gyfarwydd,' meddai, yn dal i bendroni ble roedd hi wedi gweld Ela blaen.

Cuddiodd Ela ei hwyneb y tu ôl

i'w chwrls brown, gan edrych braidd yn annifyr. 'Mae'n siŵr dy fod yn fy adnabod i – dwi'n eitha adnabyddus i rai pobl.'

Roedd Moli, Poli, Mali a Siriol ar flaen eu seddau'n methu aros i gael clywed mwy.

Y DYLWYTHEN FACH

'Ro'n i'n arfer gweithio yn Siop Swyn bob dydd Sadwrn. Dwi'n credu mod i'n cofio'ch gweld chi'n dod i mewn i brynu'r Dylwythen Fach,' ychwanegodd Ela.

'Siop Swyn!' meddai Moli, yn siomedig. 'A finnau'n meddwl dy fod ti'n enwog!'

'Ac ro'n i'n meddwl fy mod i wedi gweld dy wyneb mewn cylchgrawn yn ddiweddar,' cytunodd Mali.

Cochodd Ela. 'O-o na,' baglodd dros ei geiriau. 'Dim ond yn Siop Swyn!'

* * *

Ar ddiwedd diwrnod hir, aeth Siriol i gyfarfod ei ffrindiau wrth giât yr ysgol, fel roedden nhw'n ei wneud bob dydd.

'Beth am i ni aros am Ela,' awgrymodd Siriol, 'i weld a fyddai hi'n hoffi dod i Gaffi Seren am siocled poeth?'

'Dwi newydd ei gweld hi'n hedfan i lawr y ffordd,' meddai Moli.

'O, bechod. Ro'n i'n edrych ymlaen at gael dod i'w hadnabod hi'n well,' meddai Mali'n siomedig.

'Mi wna i drio dal i fyny gyda hi,'
meddai Siriol gan ysgwyd ei hadenydd.
'Dwi'n siŵr y byddai hi wrth ei bodd yn
dod gyda ni.' Ac ar hynny diflannodd
i chwilio am Ela.

Hedfanodd Siriol mor gyflym ag y
gallai, ond pan gyrhaeddodd waelod
y stryd, roedd Ela bron o'r golwg.
Brysiodd Siriol i droi'r gornel, jest
mewn pryd i weld Ela'n hofran i mewn
i glamp o limo gwyn!

Doedd hyn ddim yn gwneud synnwyr o gwbl, meddyliodd Siriol. Beth oedd Ela'n ei wneud mewn limo? Pam ddywedodd Brenhines y Tylwyth Teg nad oedd yn rhaid iddi sefyll ei harholiadau? Pwy oedd hi mewn gwirionedd?

'Mae gan Ela gyfrinach,' sibrydodd Siriol wrthi'i hun, 'a dwi'n benderfynol o ddarganfod y gwir!'

Gan hedfan yn ddigon uchel rhag iddi gael ei gweld, dilynodd Siriol y car hir gwyn wrth iddo yrru dros y bryniau ac i lawr y lonydd hirion. O'r diwedd, stopiodd y car y tu allan i blasty anferth yn y wlad.

Arhosodd Siriol yn dawel y tu ôl i gwmwl, gan wylio Ela'n camu allan o'r limo ac yn mynd i mewn i'r tŷ mawr. Yn sydyn, roedd Siriol yn teimlo braidd yn wirion. Ddylai hi ddim bod yn ysbïo ar ei ffrind newydd fel hyn – gallai ei holi hi

fory. Trodd i fynd, ond ar hynny
agorwyd y drws unwaith eto.

Trwyddo, cerddodd y dylwythen deg
gyda'r gwallt melyn hiraf a sythaf a
welodd Siriol erioed.

Mentrodd Siriol
hedfan yn nes i gael
gwell golwg, ond
collodd ei chydbwysedd
a chyn iddi sylweddoli
beth oedd yn
digwydd iddi,
roedd hi'n disgyn
trwy'r awyr ar
gyflymder y tu
hwnt i'w rheolaeth.

Glaniodd yn drwm
wrth draed y dylwythen deg.

Pan gododd Siriol ei phen i edrych i
fyny, roedd hi'n meddwl ei bod yn
breuddwydio.

'Waw!' meddai Siriol. Pwy oedd
yno ond Arianwen, y gantores bop

ryngwladol fwyaf llwyddiannus yn holl fyd y tylwyth teg.

'Gad i mi roi help llaw i ti,' meddai Arianwen, gan godi Siriol ar ei thraed.

Sychodd Siriol y llwch oddi ar ei dillad. 'Waw!' meddai eto, wedi'i syfrdanu'n llwyr. Arianwen oedd hoff gantores pop Siriol, a fedrai hi ddim credu ei bod hi'n sefyll yno o'i blaen hi.

'Sut galla i dy helpu di?' meddai Arianwen, â gwen ar ei hwyneb.

'Ymmm . . .' meddai Siriol, yn methu meddwl am ddim i'w ddweud.

'Dwi wedi dod i ofyn a fuasai Ela'n hoffi dod i Gaffi Seren am siocled poeth,' meddai o'r diwedd.

Edrychodd Arianwen arni mewn penbleth am eiliad. 'O, Ela!' meddai, gan chwerthin. 'Ie, Ela! Mae hi'n, ym, aros gyda fi ar y foment tra mae hi'n sefyll ei harholiadau.'

'Fyddech chi'ch dwy'n hoffi dod i Gaffi Seren?' holodd Siriol.

'Efallai y byddai hynny braidd yn anodd,' meddai Arianwen yn llawn dirgelwch. 'Does neb i fod i weld Ela a finnau gyda'n gilydd. Mae'n gyfrinach fy mod i yma o gwbl.'

'Dwi'n deall yn iawn,' meddai Siriol gan nodio'i phen yn ddifrifol. 'Wel, plîs wnei di ddweud wrthi mod i wedi galw heibio, ac y bydda i'n ei gweld hi fory yn yr ysgol?'

'Wrth gwrs,' meddai Arianwen. Cododd ei llaw wrth i Siriol hedfan i ffwrdd a'i hadenydd yn crynu mewn cyffro.

✳   ✳   ✳

'Ble buest ti mor hir?' meddai Poli pan gyrhaeddodd Siriol yng Nghaffi Seren. 'Wnest ti lwyddo i ddal i fyny ag Ela?'

Suddodd Siriol i mewn i gadair. Roedd hi wedi llwyr ymlâdd ar ôl yr holl hedfan.

'Fyddech chi ddim yn fy nghredu i hyd yn oed pe bawn i'n dweud wrthych chi, ond fedra i ddim dweud

beth bynnag am ei fod yn gyfrinach!'
meddai Siriol yn llawn dirgelwch.
Roedd hi'n gwybod y byddai cadw'r
gyfrinach yma oddi wrth ei ffrindiau'n
hynod o anodd, ond roedd yn rhaid
iddi wneud ei gorau er lles Arianwen.

'Wel, mae gennym ninnau gyfrinach
hefyd!' meddai Moli, Poli a Mali gyda'i
gilydd, gan guddio'u copi o'r
Dylwythen Fach yn sydyn, 'a fedrwn
ni ddim dweud wrthot ti!'

Roedd Siriol yn ysu am gael
gwybod beth oedd cyfrinach ei
ffrindiau, ond roedd hi'n gwybod na
fedrai hi ddweud ei chyfrinach hi
wrthyn nhw chwaith, ac felly ceisiodd
feddwl am bethau eraill.

* * *

Y diwrnod canlynol yn yr ysgol, doedd
dim angen i Siriol fynd i chwilio am
Ela. Daeth Ela o hyd iddi hi'n gyntaf.

'Rwyt ti'n edrych yn ofnadwy,'
meddai Siriol, gan sylwi ar y cysgodion
duon o dan lygaid Ela.

'Ches i ddim llawer o gwsg neithiwr,' sibrydodd Ela. 'Allwn ni fynd i rywle i siarad, yn gyfrinachol?'

Arweiniodd Siriol Ela i le cyfrinachol lle na fyddai neb yn dod o hyd iddyn nhw, sef hen dŷ gwydr ym mhen pellaf cae chwarae'r ysgol. Roedd pawb wedi hen anghofio amdano, ac roedd planhigion deiliog a mieri wedi tyfu drosto i gyd.

'Gwylia dy ben,' meddai Siriol wrth iddi greu llwybr trwy'r gwyrddni trwchus.

'Iawn,' meddai pan oedd y ddwy y tu mewn yn saff. 'Does neb yn gwybod ein bod ni yma, a does neb yn gallu ein clywed ni chwaith. Beth sy gen ti i'w ddweud?'

'O Siriol!' meddai Ela, gan ddechrau beichio crio'n sydyn. 'Mae'r wasg wedi dod i wybod

bod Arianwen yn aros yn rhywle yng nghefn gwlad ar gyrion Ffridd-las!'

'Fedra i ddim credu dy fod ti'n ei hadnabod hi!' meddai Siriol. 'Pan ddilynais i di i ofyn a hoffet ti ddod i Gaffi Seren, wnes i erioed ddychmygu y buaswn i'n cael cyfarfod ag Arianwen! Mae hi mor enwog!'

'Wnest ti ddim sôn wrth neb, naddo?' meddai Ela'n sydyn.

'Na, na! Wrth gwrs na wnes i,' meddai Siriol, wedi ei brifo braidd. Roedd hi bob amser yn ymfalchïo yn y ffaith ei bod hi'n cadw cyfrinachau'n saff.

Edrychai Ela dipyn hapusach. 'Wel,' meddai, 'mae'n gyfrinach fwy fyth nawr. Os daw'r wasg i wybod bod Arianwen yn yr ardal, yna bydd yn rhaid iddi fynd oddi yma a fydda i ddim yn cael sefyll fy arholiadau.'

'Pam bod yn rhaid i ti fynd os ydi hi'n mynd?' holodd Siriol.

Edrychodd Ela'n annifyr am foment.

'Ry'n ni'n mynd i bobman gyda'n gilydd. Does dim llawer o ffrindiau gan Arianwen gan nad yw hi'n ymddiried yn hawdd mewn pobl. Mae'n cael trafferth byw bywyd normal. Does dim byd yn breifat, ac mae popeth mae hi'n ei wneud yn cael ei gyhoeddi yn y wasg.'

Roedd dagrau mawr yn cronni yn llygaid Ela.

'Paid â phoeni, mi wna i bopeth o fewn fy ngallu i gadw dy gyfrinach yn saff,' meddai Siriol gan gofleidio Ela'n dynn.

'Diolch,' meddai Ela, cyn troi i fynd o'r tŷ gwydr. Plygodd ei phen wrth geisio mynd heibio'r tyfiant, ond cydiodd darn o ddrain yn ei gwallt.

Am eiliad, cododd y drain gwrls brown, trwchus Ela gan ddangos llond pen o wallt hir, golau! Ebychodd Siriol.

Wìg oedd gwallt Ela, ac oddi tanodd,
Arianwen oedd hi!

* * *

Doedd gan Arianwen ddim syniad fod
Siriol yn gwybod pwy oedd hi go
iawn, ond am yr ychydig wythnosau
nesaf yn yr ysgol, gwnaeth Siriol
bopeth o fewn ei gallu i gadw
cyfrinach ei ffrind yn saff.

Pan glywai dylwyth teg eraill yn
trafod pam tybed ei bod hi'n edrych
mor gyfarwydd, llwyddodd Siriol i'w
darbwyllo mai yn Siop Swyn roedden
nhw wedi'i gweld hi.

Pan oedd newyddiadurwyr yn gofyn
cwestiynau yng Nghaffi Seren, byddai
Siriol yn llwyddo i dynnu'u sylw gan
ddweud celwydd ei bod wedi gweld
Arianwen ar Ynys yr Adar.

Pan fyddai wìg Ela'n symud, roedd
Siriol yn llwyddo i'w dynnu'n ôl i'w le
heb i neb sylwi, ddim hyd yn oed Ela
ei hun!

* * *

Pan ddaeth hi'n amser i Ela sefyll yr arholiadau, roedd Siriol wrth ei bodd eu bod nhw wedi llwyddo i gadw'r gyfrinach yn saff, ond roedd hi hefyd yn teimlo'n drist gan y byddai ei ffrind newydd yn ei gadael.

'Fe fydda i'n dy golli di,' meddai Ela wrth Siriol wrth iddyn nhw ffarwelio. 'Rwyt ti wedi bod yn ffrind da iawn i mi, ac yn bwysicach fyth, yn ffrind dwi'n gallu ymddiried ynddi.'

'Ac yn ffrind i Arianwen!' meddai Siriol, yn gwybod y gwir.

'Rwyt ti'n gwybod?' meddai Arianwen wedi'i synnu.

'Ers hydoedd!' meddai Siriol, gan chwerthin. 'Ond dwi wedi cadw dy gyfrinach di'n saff.'

'Wel, nawr fy mod i wedi sefyll fy arholiadau does dim rhaid cadw'r gyfrinach o hyn ymlaen,' meddai Arianwen, gan dynnu'r wìg oddi ar ei phen a gadael i'w gwallt hir golau ddisgyn yn rhydd.

Roedd yr holl dylwyth teg o'u cwmpas wedi sefyll yn eu hunfan ac yn syllu ar Arianwen. Fedrai Siriol ddim peidio â chwerthin wrth weld y syndod ar eu hwynebau pan sylweddolodd pawb fod Ela yn neb llai na'r seren bop fyd-enwog!

* * *

'Mae gen i rywbeth anhygoel i'w ddweud wrthych chi,' meddai Siriol wrth iddi ymuno â Moli, Poli a Mali ar ôl yr ysgol. 'Roedd Ela'n gwisgo wìg i guddio'r ffaith mai'r seren bop enwog Arianwen oedd hi go iawn!'

'O, roeddet ti'n gwybod?' meddai Moli wedi'i synnu. 'Wnaethon ni ddim dweud wrthyt ti achos roedden ni'n meddwl y byddet ti'n dweud wrth bawb!'

'Beth y'ch chi'n feddwl?' meddai Siriol wedi drysu. 'Roeddech chi'n gwybod?'

'Fe wnaethon ni ffeindio allan y diwrnod hwnnw pan wnest ti ofyn i Ela ddod gyda ni i Gaffi Seren,' meddai Mali. 'Roedd 'na erthygl gyfan yn Y Dylwythen Fach am sut oedd Arianwen eisiau sefyll ei harholiadau a'i bod wedi symud i rywle yn ymyl Ffridd-las!'

'Pan welson ni'r llun, y cyfan oedd angen ei wneud oedd tynnu llun o gyrls ar ei gwallt ac fe wnaethon ni ei hadnabod hi'n syth,' esboniodd Poli.

'Ond sonioch chi 'run gair,' meddai Siriol mewn sioc.

'Wnest tithau ddim chwaith!' meddai'r gweddill yn un côr.

'Wel, mae'n debyg mai dyna sy'n gwneud cyfrinach yn gyfrinach!' meddai Siriol gan chwerthin.

Sialens y Siocled

'Iawn, dwi'n cytuno!' meddai Siriol
Swyn yn hyderus wrth ei ffrindiau gan
ysgwyd llaw â phob un yn eu tro.

Roedd Moli, Poli a Mali bron yn siŵr
y byddai'n amhosibl i Siriol roi'r gorau
i fwyta siocled, ond roedd Siriol yn
benderfynol o'u profi'n anghywir!
Roedd y tylwyth teg wedi penderfynu
rhoi'r gorau i fwyta siocled am fis cyfan.

'Rwyt ti *yn* sylweddoli fod dim
siocled yn golygu dim diod siocled
poeth chwaith?' meddai Poli, gan
wneud y rheolau'n glir.

'Nac ysgytlaeth siocled chwaith,' meddai Mali.

'Ddim hyd yn oed gwm cnoi siocled,' meddai Moli.

'Iawn, iawn!' meddai Siriol yn benderfynol. 'Rwy'n siŵr y galla i wneud hyn,' meddai, gan swnio'n fwy hyderus nag roedd hi'n teimlo mewn gwirionedd.

'Chaiff yr un darn lleiaf o siocled fynd heibio'n gwefusau ni am fis cyfan, neu fe fydd yn rhaid i ni rannu'r gyfrinach fwyaf sy ganddon ni!' meddai Poli.

Gwingodd Siriol. Roedd ganddi hi sawl cyfrinach, ond doedd hi ddim yn awyddus i'w rhannu nhw gyda phawb.

✴ ✴ ✴

Roedd rhoi'r gorau i fwyta siocled yn fwy anodd nag roedd Siriol erioed wedi'i ddychmygu. Erbyn y trydydd diwrnod, nid yn unig roedd hi'n breuddwydio am siocled yn y nos, ond roedd siocled ar ei meddwl bron bob munud o'r dydd hefyd!

'Beth ydi hwn?' meddai Miss Pefriog, yr athrawes gemeg, pan ddaeth i edrych ar waith Siriol.

'Llwch pefriog gradd dau, Miss,' meddai Siriol, gan edrych i lawr ar y gronynnau disglair yn ei dysgl.

'Nage wir, Siriol. Powdr siocled o'r radd flaenaf ydi hwn,' meddai Miss Pefriog gan roi ei bys ynddo ac yna ei lyfu.

'Pan wyt ti'n creu rhywbeth hudol, mae'n rhaid i ti ganolbwyntio. Mae'r hyn sy ar dy feddwl di'n siŵr o effeithio ar beth wyt ti'n ei greu. Rho gynnig arall arni, os gweli di'n dda, Siriol, a'r tro yma rhaid i ti gadw dy feddwl ar dy waith.'

Dechreuodd Siriol ar yr arbrawf eto. Roedd hi'n teimlo'n benisel.

Edrychodd Moli, Poli a Mali ar ei gilydd yr ochr arall i'r dosbarth. Erbyn hyn roedden nhw'n fwy sicr nag erioed na fyddai Siriol yn gallu cadw'i gair.

* * *

Doedd pethau'n ddim haws yn y gwersi eraill chwaith.

Roedd lefel egni Siriol yn y gwersi chwaraeon lawer yn is heb ei bar o siocled Sglein arferol amser cinio i roi hwb iddi. Yn y wers mathemateg roedd yn rhaid iddyn nhw gyfrif botymau siocled, a bu bron i'r temtasiwn fod yn ormod i Siriol.

ffon hud
siocled

A doedd y bisgedi
siocled y bu'n eu
pobi yn y wers
goginio ddim yn blasu'r
un fath heb siocled
ynddyn nhw!

Ar ddiwedd
yr wythnos gyntaf, roedd Siriol bron
â drysu'n lân heb siocled. Gwelai
siocled ym mhob man roedd hi'n
edrych – trodd y bryniau'n gacennau
siocled, trodd yr haul yn fisged siocled
fawr, a'r afonydd yn siocled poeth!

'Fydd neb ddim callach,' meddai
wrthi'i hun wrth iddi hofran i'r gegin a
chwilio drwy ei 'drôr melys'. Roedd
honno'n llawn dop o bob math o
siocled. Glafoeriodd Siriol dros y
siocled tywyll o wlad Belg roedd hi
wedi bod yn ei gadw at achlysur
arbennig. Arogleuodd y jar o bowdr
coco cryf, a dychmygu'i hun yn swatio
yn y gadair freichiau gyda chwpanaid o
siocled poeth. Ac er eu bod nhw'n fach

iawn, byddai'r siafins siocled yn fwy na digon i roi stop ar ei blys am siocled.

Digon oedd digon! Caeodd Siriol y llenni'n gyflym, a gwneud yn siŵr nad oedd neb y tu allan i'r drws ffrynt. Edrychodd dros ei hysgwyddau ac yna, yn ara deg bach, rhwygodd y papur oedd am y siocled, gan drysori'r foment, ac yna rhoi'r sgwaryn siocled yn ei cheg. Roedd yn hyfryd!

Doedd Siriol ddim wedi bwriadu twyllo, ond roedd hi'n gwybod ei bod hi wedi cyrraedd y pen. Wrth gyfrif yn ei phen, gwyddai y byddai un sgwaryn bychan bach o siocled y dydd yn ddigon i'w chadw i fynd tan ddiwedd y mis, a doedd hynny ddim yn rhy ddrwg, oedd e? Cyfrifodd ddigon o sgwariau siocled ar gyfer cael un bob dydd tan ddiwedd y mis, a'u gosod yn y lle mwyaf cyfrinachol oedd ganddi – ei Bocs Cyfrinachau.

✳ ✳ ✳

'Mae Siriol i weld yn ymdopi'n dda iawn heb siocled yr wythnos yma,' meddai Poli wrth Moli a Mali.

Roedd Poli eisiau bod yn dylwythen deg y dannedd rhyw ddiwrnod, felly doedd ganddi hi ddim dant melys, a doedd hi ddim yn cael llawer o drafferth wrth gadw at yr her. Roedd Moli a Mali'n ei chael hi'n anodd iawn, ond fydden nhw byth yn cyfaddef hynny o flaen Poli.

'Ydi,' cytunodd Mali. 'Efallai ei bod hi wedi dod dros ei hobsesiwn gyda siocled erbyn hyn.'

'Oni bai ei bod hi'n twyllo!' meddai Moli'n ddrwgdybus. 'Dwi'n meddwl y dylen ni alw heibio fel syrpreis i wneud yn siŵr.'

'Fedrwn ni ddim gwneud hynny!' meddai Poli, wedi'i syfrdanu. 'Dwi'n siŵr na fyddai Siriol yn twyllo. Rydyn ni bob amser yn gwneud pob dim gyda'n gilydd a dydi hyn ddim yn eithriad.'

'Beth am i ni alw heibio i ddweud "helô" 'te?' meddai Mali, a oedd yn tueddu i gytuno nad oedd gan Siriol lawer o hunanreolaeth ar y gorau.

* * *

Yn ffodus i Siriol, roedd hi newydd lyncu ei darn bach dyddiol o siocled pan gerddodd Moli, Poli a Mali drwy'r drws cefn yn ddirybudd.

'O helô!' meddai Siriol, gan gochi mewn euogrwydd. 'Am syrpreis neis!'

'Gobeithio nad wyt ti'n meindio ein bod ni wedi galw heibio i dy weld di fel hyn, ond roedden ni'n digwydd pasio,' meddai Poli, gan sylwi bod y llenni wedi'u cau. 'Mae hi braidd yn dywyll mewn fan hyn.'

'Ym, ydi,' meddai Siriol, gan roi ei Bocs Cyfrinachau yn ôl yn y drôr yn frysiog. 'Ro'n i'n teimlo braidd yn flinedig ac yn meddwl mynd i'r gwely am ychydig.' Roedd yn gas gan Siriol ddweud celwydd wrth ei ffrindiau, ond doedd hi ddim eisiau eu siomi nhw gyda'r gwir chwaith.

'Ond mae hi'n ganol y pnawn,' meddai Moli yn amheus.

'Dwi'n meddwl mai'r diffyg siocled sydd ar fai,' meddai Siriol, yn falch ei bod wedi meddwl am gystal ateb mor gyflym.

'Wel, byddai'n well i ni fynd, felly, er mwyn i ti gael llonydd i gysgu,' awgrymodd Poli. 'Paid â phoeni am ddod at y drws gyda ni.'

Yn erbyn ei hewyllys, ffarweliodd Siriol â'i ffrindiau a throi am ei hystafell wely. Byddai'n well o lawer ganddi dreulio'i hamser gyda'i ffrindiau nag yn y tŷ ar ei phen ei hun.

✳   ✳   ✳

'Dwi ddim yn meddwl ei bod hi'n twyllo,' meddai Mali wrth iddyn nhw baratoi i fynd.

'Nac ydi, ddim a hithau wedi blino yn y pnawn,' meddai Poli, oedd wedi credu stori Siriol.

'Fe fyddai 'na dystiolaeth i'w weld pe bai hi wedi bod yn bwyta siocled ar y slei,' meddai Moli, gan blygu i lawr i estyn ei bag. 'FEL HWN!' meddai a dangos darn o bapur aur oddi ar far o siocled.

Chymerodd hi fawr o amser iddyn nhw weld o ble daeth y papur aur. Roedd 'na un drôr yn gilagored gan ei bod yn orlawn oherwydd Bocs Cyfrinachol Siriol.

'Fedra i ddim credu ei bod hi'n twyllo!' ebychodd Mali.

'Ro'n i'n gwybod na fyddai hi'n llwyddo,' meddai Moli, yn wên o glust i glust. 'Dydi pawb ddim mor gryf a phenderfynol â fi.'

Roedd Poli wedi'i siomi gyda

Siriol. 'Y peth gorau fedrwn ni ei wneud er mwyn helpu Siriol fyddai cuddio'r siocled yma'n rhywle arall. Yna'r tro nesaf y bydd hi'n awchu am siocled, fydd 'na ddim siocled o gwmpas y lle,' meddai Poli, gan gau'r caead yn gyflym a rhoi'r bocs yn ei bag.

Aeth y tylwyth teg allan o'r tŷ yn dawel drwy'r drws cefn a throi tuag adref.

* * *

Ar ôl ysgol y diwrnod canlynol, gwrthododd Siriol y cynnig i fynd i Gaffi Seren am wydryn o ysgytlaeth. Yn hytrach, aeth yn syth adref ac i'w drôr melys i nôl y sgwaryn o siocled oedd wedi bod ar ei meddwl drwy'r dydd. Roedd hi wedi bod yn edrych ymlaen gymaint at y foment yma. Rhewodd yn ei hunfan – ble oedd ei Bocs Cyfrinachau!? Roedd hi'n sicr ei bod wedi'i roi'n ôl yn y drôr ddoe, ond roedd e wedi diflannu!

Aeth drwy pob ystafell yn y tŷ gan chwilio ym mhob cwpwrdd a phob drôr, ac o dan bob dodrefnyn hyd nes ei bod yn hollol sicr nad oedd y Bocs Cyfrinachau yn y tŷ.

'Beth wna i?' gwichiodd Siriol yn uchel, yn poeni'n ofnadwy. Nid yn unig roedd ei chyflenwad cyfrinachol o siocled yn y bocs, ond yno hefyd roedd Siriol yn cadw'i holl gyfrinachau ei hun! Roedd hi'n ysgrifennu pob cyfrinach oedd ganddi, yn ei llawysgrifen orau un, ar ddarn bychan bach o bapur ac yn ei gadw yn ei bocs.

Roedd y syniad bod rhywun yn darllen ei chyfrinachau yn ormod iddi, a'r noson honno fedrai hi ddim cysgu winc.

'Ble mae'r Bocs Cyfrinachau?' mwmiodd wrth iddi droi a throsi yn ei

gwely. 'Beth petai rywun yn dod
o hyd i'r bocs ac yn ei agor?!' meddai'n
uchel gan eistedd i fyny'n syth yn y
gwely. 'Fyddai'r holl gyfrinachau pwysig
yna ddim yn gyfrinachau mwyach.
A beth petai e neu hi ddim yn gallu
cadw cyfrinach ac yn dweud wrth
rywun arall?' Roedd hyn yn
anobeithiol. Doedd gan Siriol ddim
gobaith gallu ymlacio na chysgu tra
bod y Bocs Cyfrinachau ar goll.

* * *

Erbyn i Poli gyrraedd tŷ Siriol y
diwrnod canlynol er mwyn cerdded
i'r ysgol gyda hi, roedd Sirol yn
teimlo'n swp sâl ar ôl poeni drwy'r
nos.

'Beth ar wyneb daear y tylwyth teg
wyt ti wedi bod yn ei wneud?' meddai
Poli, gan ddringo dros gynnwys cegin
Siriol a oedd erbyn hyn wedi'i wasgaru
dros ei gardd. Ymddangosodd Siriol
allan o bentwr o offer cegin, a golwg
wyllt a blinedig arni.

'Dwi wedi colli rhywbeth cyfrinachol, ac mae'n rhaid i mi ddod o hyd iddo. Fedra i ddim stopio nes fy mod i'n ei gael yn ôl!' meddai Siriol gan chwilio a chwalu'n orffwyll drwy ddrôr roedd hi eisoes wedi edrych ynddi ddegau o weithiau!

'Fedra i helpu?' mentrodd Poli, yn teimlo'n reit euog am ei bod yn gwybod yn iawn am beth oedd Siriol yn chwilio, a ble'r oedd e.

'Na, na. Mae'r hyn dwi wedi'i golli'n gyfrinachol. A dweud y gwir mae e'n llawn cyfrinachau, a fi ydi'r unig un all ddod o hyd iddo.'

Cododd Poli. 'Wyt ti'n siŵr fod beth bynnag rwyt ti wedi ei golli'n gymaint o gyfrinach fel na fedri di ei rhannu?' holodd Poli, yn ceisio helpu Siriol i gyfaddef ei bod hi wedi bod yn bwyta siocled.

'O mae'n gyfrinach rhy fawr o lawer i'w rhannu,' meddai Siriol, gan ddal ymlaen i chwilio.

'Byddai'n well i mi fynd, felly, er mwyn i ti gael llonydd,' meddai Poli gan hedfan i ffwrdd. 'Paid â bod yn hwyr i'r ysgol.'

* * *

Amser chwarae, galwodd Poli am gyfarfod brys o dan y Dderwen Fawr yn y cae.

'Mae gen i ofn bod chwarae wedi troi'n chwerw,' meddai'n ddifrifol wrth Moli a Mali. 'Dydi Siriol ddim yn gallu ymdopi heb siocled. Fe es i heibio'i thŷ hi ac roedd popeth dros y lle i gyd!'

'Beth wyt ti'n ei feddwl?' meddai Mali'n bryderus.

'Mae Siriol wedi troi'r tŷ wyneb i waered yn chwilio am ei siocled. Ro'n i wirioneddol yn meddwl ein bod ni'n gwneud y peth iawn wrth ei guddio oddi wrthi, ond nawr dydw i ddim mor siŵr,' meddai Poli, gan agor ei bag a thynnu'r Bocs Cyfrinachol ohono.

'O na!' ebychodd Mali. 'Mae'n rhaid ei bod hi'n cael amser caled iawn.'

'Ond dim ond pythefnos sydd wedi mynd heibio,' cwynodd Moli. 'A dwi wedi bod yn cael hwyl dda iawn.'

'Wir nawr,' pwysleisiodd Poli, 'petaech chi wedi gweld Siriol, byddech chi'n meddwl yr un fath â fi. Mae'n rhaid i ni roi'r bocs yn ôl iddi.'

* * *

Pan gyrhaeddodd y tylwyth teg dŷ Siriol ar ôl ysgol, doedd dim golwg o Siriol yn unman.

Chwiliodd y tair ym mhobman hyd nes i Mali ddod o hyd iddi o'r diwedd yn cysgu o dan sinc y gegin!

Yn dawel, dringodd y tair dros y llanast a'i deffro'n dyner.

'Siriol, deffra. Mae dy focs di fan

hyn!' meddai Mali, gan ysgwyd Siriol
yn ysgafn i'w deffro.

Yn gysglyd, agorodd Siriol ei llygaid
a bu bron iddi grio pan welodd ei
Bocs Cyfrinachau.

'Ble daethoch chi o hyd iddo fe?'
gofynnodd, gan godi ar ei heistedd a
rhwbio'i llygaid. 'Sut oeddech chi'n
gwybod mai dyma beth o'n i'n chwilio

amdano?' holodd wedyn, wedi drysu'n lan.

'Ni gymerodd e, ac mae'n ddrwg iawn ganddon ni. Roedden ni'n meddwl ein bod yn gwneud y peth iawn,' meddai Poli.

'Mae dy gyfrinachau di'n saff gyda ni,' meddai Moli.

Roedd Siriol ar bigau'r drain. Doedd hi ddim yn ddelfrydol fod ei ffrindiau'n gwybod ei holl gyfrinachau, ond o leiaf gallai ymddiried yn Moli, Poli a Mali i beidio â dweud gair wrth unrhyw un arall.

'Chwarae teg i chi,' meddai Siriol. 'Mae cyfrinachau fel y rhain yn rhai anodd i'w cadw'n saff. Ydych chi'n addo na wnewch chi fyth ddweud wrth yr un dylwythen deg arall?'

'Wrth gwrs ein bod ni,' meddai Poli gan ei chysuro.

'Yn bendant,' meddai Mali.

'Wel, os ydi e'n golygu gymaint

â hynny i ti nad oes neb yn dod i wybod dy fod di wedi twyllo yn ein her ddi-siocled ni, yna mae hynny'n iawn gyda fi,' meddai Moli. 'Ond yn bersonol dwi'n meddwl dy fod ti wedi ymateb ychydig dros ben llestri.'

'Ond beth am y gyfrinach fy mod i'n caru'r pâr o deits streipiog sy gen i gymaint nes fy mod i weithiau'n eu gwisgo nhw yn fy ngwely?' holodd Siriol yn boenus.

Edrychodd Moli, Poli a Mali ar ei gilydd mewn penbleth.

'A'r un am y llyfr o'r llyfrgell – "Sut i fod yn Ffrind Gorau" – y gwnes i ei fenthyg fisoedd yn ôl ac sy'n dal heb ei ddychwelyd? A beth am rysáit fy nghacennau hud? Ydych chi'n addo peidio â dweud wrth neb am y cynhwysyn cyfrinachol sydd gen i, sef y pum-sbeis hud i roi ychydig o gic i'r gymysgedd?' byrlymodd Siriol gan siarad yn ddi-stop.

O'r diwedd
rhoddodd Siriol
y gorau i restru'i
chyfrinachau mwyaf,
a sylwi am y tro cyntaf bod ei ffrindiau
yn rowlio chwerthin ar y llawr.

'O Siriol, does dim syndod fod dy
gacennau di'n blasu mor rhyfedd!'
meddai Poli, gan gofleidio'i ffrind.

Edrychai Siriol Swyn ar goll, braidd,
ac yna agorodd gaead y Bocs
Cyfrinachau'n araf. Roedd ei
chyfrinachau'n dal yno, yn swatio'n
ddwfn yng ngwaelod y bocs.

'Wnaethoch chi mo'u darllen
nhw?!' meddai, gan sylweddoli'n sydyn
ei bod wedi gwneud camgymeriad.

'Naddo, siŵr iawn!' meddai ei
ffrindiau'n un côr. 'Dy gyfrinachau
di oedden nhw.'

'Wel, os felly, mae'n edrych yn
debyg bod yr her ar ben!' meddai
Moli, gan gofio'r rheolau a osodwyd
ar y dechrau. 'Dwi'n meddwl ein bod

ni i gyd yn gwybod mai dy gyfrinach fwyaf di ydi'r ffaith dy fod di'n Siocaholic!'

Gall y cyfrinachau rwyt ti'n ofni eu datgelu

arwain at syrpreis annisgwyl wrth i ti eu rhannu.

Gweld y Gwir

Roedd Siriol Swyn yn poeni. Fory oedd diwrnod y Prawf Swyn Blynyddol yn Ysgol y Naw Dymuniad, ac roedd hi'n ofni y byddai hi'n methu'n druenus.

'Dwi ddim yn dda iawn am greu swyn,' meddai Siriol, gan chwarae gyda blaen ei ffon hud.

'Dydi hynny ddim yn wir,' meddai Mali. 'Rwyt ti angen ychydig mwy o ymarfer, dyna'r cyfan.'

'Ond dydi e ddim yn dod yn naturiol i mi,' meddai Siriol yn ddigalon.

'Dydi e ddim yn dod yn naturiol i neb,' meddai Poli, gan geisio codi calon Siriol. 'Dydi'r ffaith ein bod ni'n dylwyth teg ddim yn golygu ein bod ni wastad yn gallu creu swyn.'

'Ond mae Arabela ac Anna'n gallu,' meddai Moli, gan bwyntio i gyfeiriad dwy dylwythen deg a edrychai bron yn union yr un fath. Roedd y ddwy'n ymarfer chwyrlïo eu ffyn hud ar ochr arall y cae chwarae.

Roedd Arabela ac Anna mor debyg nes bod y tylwyth teg eraill wedi meddwl mai gefeilliaid oedden nhw.

Mewn gwirionedd, ffrindiau gorau oedden nhw – ffrindiau gorau oedd yn gwneud popeth gyda'i gilydd: roedden nhw'n siopa gyda'i gilydd am ddillad yn union yr un fath, roedden nhw'n copïo steil gwallt

ei gilydd, ac roedden nhw hyd yn
yn oed yn rhannu'r un llawysgrifen!

Y peth mwyaf anhygoel amdanyn
nhw, fodd bynnag, oedd y ffaith fod
y ddwy'n gallu creu swyn yn gwbl
naturiol.

Hyd yn oed yn eu gwers swyn
gyntaf un yn Ysgol y Naw Dymuniad
roedd Miss Pŵer, yr athrawes swyn,
wedi'i synnu gan eu gallu.

'Efallai y gofynna i iddyn nhw am
gyngor,' meddai Siriol, gan wylio'n
geg-agored wrth i sêr swyn perffaith
hedfan o'u ffyn mewn patrwm pert.

'Pob lwc i ti,' chwarddodd Moli.
'Wnaiff Arabela ac Anna fyth rannu
cyfrinach eu llwyddiant gyda neb.'

Ochneidiodd Siriol. Efallai na fyddai
hi fyth yn un dda am greu swyn.

* * *

Erbyn diwedd y dydd, pan ddaeth yr amser iddi fynd adref, roedd nerfau Siriol wedi cael y gorau ohoni. Lle bynnag yr edrychai, roedd yno dylwyth teg yn chwifio'u ffyn hud ac yn creu effeithiau anhygoel, wrth iddyn nhw ymarfer at y gystadleuaeth. Ond allai Siriol ddim hyd yn oed greu'r swyn symlaf heb i bopeth fynd o chwith! Doedd ganddi ddim dewis arall ond gofyn i Arabela ac Anna am help.

'Helô,' meddai Siriol, gan alw i mewn i'r ystafell ddosbarth wag. 'Oes rhywun yma?'

Roedd Arabela ac Anna wastad yn aros ar ôl ysgol yn y dosbarth cemeg, yn creu pob math o lwch pefriog newydd. Roedden nhw'n gobeithio y bydden nhw un diwrnod yn ennill Gwobr Gwyddoniaeth y Flwyddyn i Dylwyth Teg.

'O!' gwichiodd Anna, a bu bron iddi ollwng y pot pefriog oedd yn ei llaw. 'Siriol Swyn wyt ti, yntê?'

'Ie,' meddai Siriol. 'Ond dydi fy enw i'n fawr o help i mi greu swyn, chwaith.'

'Wel, mae'r Prawf Swyn Blynyddol fory, felly byddai'n well i ti ddechrau ymarfer!' chwarddodd Anna wrth iddi dywallt ychydig o lwch pefriog i'r bicer mawr byrlymog o'i blaen.

'A dweud y gwir, dyna pam rydw i yma,' meddai Siriol yn swil. 'Ble mae Arabela?'

'Mae hi wedi mynd adref i orffwys ei braich yn barod at fory. Fe wnaeth hi ei throi wrth wneud swyn cawod enfys ddwbl y prynhawn yma.'

Ochneidiodd Siriol. Gwyddai ei bod yn annhebygol iawn y gallai hi greu swyn syml hyd yn oed, heb sôn am swyn cawod enfys ddwbl!

'Ro'n i'n meddwl tybed a fyddet ti'n gallu rhoi ychydig o gyngor i mi ar sut i greu swyn?' gofynnodd Siriol yn obeithiol.

Stopiodd Anna am eiliad gan roi ei bicer i lawr. 'Pa mor wael yn union wyt ti?' holodd yn chwilfrydig.

Estynnodd Siriol ei ffon hud, rhoi ei bag i lawr a dangos ei chwifiad gorau i Anna.

'Mmm,' meddai Anna, gan godi'i haeliau a gwneud ei gorau i feddwl am ffordd garedig o fod yn onest. 'Dwi'n meddwl bod gen ti le i wella, ond, yn anffodus, rwyt ti wedi'i gadael hi braidd yn hwyr i ymarfer.'

'O, paid â phoeni,' meddai Siriol, gan geisio peidio â swnio'n rhy siomedig. 'Does dim dewis arall ond gwneud fy ngorau glas ar y diwrnod. Diolch i ti, beth bynnag.' Cododd Siriol ei bag yn araf a throi i fynd.

'Aros!' galwodd Anna cyn i Siriol gyrraedd y drws. 'Fedri di gadw cyfrinach?'

Trodd Siriol yn ei hôl yn syth. Roedd hi wrth ei bodd gyda chyfrinachau. 'Gallaf,' atebodd yn onest.

'Rho bum munud i mi glirio fan hyn, ac fe af i â ti i rywle lle gelli di chwifio dy ffon yn y ffordd fwyaf sylfaenol ac ennill marciau llawn mewn munudau!'

✳ ✳ ✳

Hedfanodd Anna a Siriol allan o Ysgol y Naw Dymuniad, dros gaeau chwarae'r ysgol ac ar hyd llwybr hir a throellog hyd nes iddyn nhw gyrraedd Coedwig y Naw Dymuniad.

Ymhell yng nghanol y coed roedd yr unig le yn Nhre'r Blodau lle tyfai sêr-flodau arian. Y paill oedd y

cynhwysyn pwysig mewn pob math o
lwch pefriog gan ei fod yn cynnwys
nodweddion hudol.

Erbyn i Siriol ag Anna gyrraedd y
coed roedd hi wedi tywyllu, a'r unig
sŵn i'w glywed oedd siffrwd y dail.

'Ble wyt ti?' sibrydodd Siriol, gan
ymestyn ei llaw i'r tywyllwch.

'Dwi draw fan hyn,' meddai Anna
gan biffian chwerthin, a chynnau tortsh
bychan.

Roedd golau'r tortsh yn taflu cysgodion rhyfedd o'u cwmpas.

'Sut mae hyn yn mynd i wella fy sgiliau chwifio?' gofynnodd Siriol, gan deimlo braidd yn anesmwyth yn y tywyllwch.

'Dilyna fi ac fe ddangosaf i ti,' meddai Anna wrth iddi droedio'n ysgafn tuag at fonyn bedwen fawr.

Aeth Siriol ar ôl Anna draw at y goeden. 'Am beth rydyn ni'n chwilio?' holodd Siriol. Roedd ei bol yn swnian am fwyd, a hithau'n difaru peidio â mynd yn syth adref i gael te.

'Shhhh!' meddai Anna, gan godi'i bys at ei gwefusau a defnyddio'r tortsh i edrych ar ei wats. 'Unrhyw funud nawr!'

Yn sydyn, ffrwydrodd y sêr-flodau arian yn agored i ddatgelu petalau prydferth, a'r rheiny'n disgleirio â llwch pefriog. Safai Siriol yn gegagored yn rhyfeddu at yr olygfa – doedd hi erioed wedi gweld unrhyw beth mor brydferth â hyn o'r blaen.

Yn sydyn, gafaelodd Anna yn ffon
hud Siriol a'i thapio'n ysgafn yng
nghanol un o'r blodau.
Yna gwnaeth yr un
peth gyda'i ffon
hud ei hun.

Caeodd y petalau cyn gyflymed ag yr
agoron nhw.

'Waw!' meddai Siriol, gan edrych yn
ofalus ar y pelydrau oedd yn
amgylchynu ei ffon hud. Doedd dim
angen defnyddio tortsh Anna erbyn hyn.

'Mae e'n syfrdanol, on'd ydi e?' meddai Anna. 'Tyrd yn dy flaen!' meddai'n gyffrous, 'rho gynnig ar chwifio dy ffon hud di nawr!'

Safodd Siriol yn nerfus, gan osod ei thraed yn gadarn, cau ei llygaid, canolbwyntio ar ei dymuniad, a chwifio'i ffon hud gyda'i holl nerth.

'WAW!' meddai Siriol yn uwch na'r tro diwethaf hyd yn oed. 'Roedd fel petai'r ffon hud yn ei chwifio'i hun!'

'Ac roedd hi gant y cant yn berffaith!' meddai Anna. 'Fedrai hyd yn oed y dylwythen deg fwyaf profiadol ddim bod wedi cael gwell hwyl arni.'

* * *

Ar y ffordd 'nôl, eglurodd Anna wrth Siriol nad oedd hi bob amser wedi defnyddio'r sêr-flodau arian i'w helpu gyda dymuniadau. Sawl blwyddyn yn ôl, roedd Arabela a hithau wedi cofrestru ar gyfer cystadleuaeth ryngwladol ac roedd pwysau mawr arnyn nhw i lwyddo. Perfformiodd

Arabela ei swyn heb broblem, fel arfer, ond roedd nerfau wedi cael y gorau o Anna. Cyn iddi sylweddoli, roedd hi wedi gollwng ei ffon hud yn ystod rhan mwyaf tyngedfennol y prawf.

Roedd methiant Anna i ennill marciau sylfaenol, hyd yn oed, wedi gwneud iddi deimlo fel petai wedi siomi pawb – ei ffrind gorau, yr ysgol, Miss Pŵer, a phawb yn Nhre'r Blodau!

'Roedd e'n ofnadwy,' meddai Anna. 'Fe wnes i addo i mi fy hun na fyddwn i byth eto'n creu swyn ar lefel gystadleuol, ac er i Arabela a Miss Pŵer geisio helpu, ddaeth fy hyder i fyth yn ôl . . . nes i mi grwydro i'r coed un diwrnod a dod ar draws y sêr-flodau arian.'

Edrychodd Siriol yn syn. 'Beth? Wyt ti'n defnyddio'r llwch hud mewn cystadlaethau nawr?'

'Bob tro!' meddai Anna. 'Ond paid â dweud wrth neb; dydi hyd yn oed Arabela ddim yn gwybod. Mae hi'n meddwl fy mod i wedi cael fy hyder a'm gallu'n ôl oherwydd ei help hi, nid oherwydd y llwch hud.'

Edrychodd Siriol i lawr ar ei ffon

belydrol. 'Pa mor hir mae effaith y llwch yn debygol o bara?' gofynnodd.

'Am ddeuddeg awr,' meddai Anna. 'Os wyt ti'n bwriadu ei ddefnyddio ar gyfer y prawf, yna fe fydd yn rhaid i ti nôl mwy fory.' Ac ar hynny hedfanodd Anna i'r tywyllwch, gan adael Siriol yn syllu ar ei ffon euraidd.

* * *

Y noson honno gorweddodd Siriol ar ddihun yn poeni, ac am y tro cyntaf yr wythnos honno doedd hi ddim yn poeni am ei phrawf swyn ei hun. Roedd hi'n poeni bod hyder Anna'n dibynnu'n hollol ar y llwch hud o'r sêr-flodau arian. Bu Anna unwaith yn naturiol dda am greu swyni, ac roedd Siriol yn sicr y gallai fod felly eto – petai hi ond yn credu ynddi hi'i hun.

* * *

Y diwrnod canlynol yn yr ysgol, aeth Siriol i gyfarfod Moli, Poli a Mali o dan y Dderwen Fawr.

'Wyt ti'n barod am y prawf?'

gofynnodd Poli. 'Gest ti rywfaint o gyngor gan Anna?'

'Do a naddo,' meddai Siriol yn lletchwith.

'Wel?' meddai Mali'n gyffrous. 'Wyt ti'n gwybod beth yw cyfrinach fawr swynwraig fwyaf talentog yr ysgol?'

Meddyliodd Siriol yn ofalus am foment.

'Hyder,' meddai. 'Dyna ydi'r cynhwysyn mwyaf hudol yn y byd!'

'Hawdd iddi hi ddweud hynny,' meddai Moli. 'Mae hyder yn dod gyda llwyddiant, ac mae'n rhaid i mi gyfaddef bod hynny'n eitha prin i ni'n pedair!'

'Ddim o angenrheidrwydd,' meddai Siriol yn ofalus. 'Os byddwn ni i gyd yn annog ein gilydd, a chredu, fe ddaw llwyddiant yn ei sgil.'

Adleisiai geiriau Siriol yn ei phen ei hun, ac yn sydyn fe gafodd hi syniad ardderchog! 'Mae'n rhaid i mi fynd!' meddai gan edrych ar y cloc.

'Fe wela i chi yn y prawf yn nes ymlaen.'

* * *

Hedfanodd Siriol mor gyflym ag y gallai. Gwyddai na fedrai hi fyth fradychu ffydd Anna drwy ddweud wrth Frenhines y Tylwyth Teg, Miss Pŵer, na hyd yn oed wrth Arabela, beth oedd ei chyfrinach. Ond gallai wneud rhywbeth arall, a phetai hynny'n gweithio, yna ni fyddai'n rhaid i Anna gadw'i chyfrinach yn saff.

'Tyrd â dy ffon hud di i mi,' sibrydodd Siriol wrth Anna yn y ciw

amser cinio. 'Dwi'n picio i "ti'n-gwybod-ble" ac fe wnaf i dy ffon di ar yr un pryd, os hoffet ti?'

'Diolch, Siriol,' meddai Anna gan wenu. 'Ro'n i wedi gobeithio gadael fy ngwers nesaf yn fuan er mwyn hedfan yno fy hun. Gwna'n siŵr dy fod ti'n cael digon o lwch arni – dwi wirioneddol eisiau i'r prawf yma fynd yn dda!'

Winciodd Siriol a chodi llaw ar Anna. 'Wela i di'n nes mlaen!' meddai a diflannu mewn chwinciad.

'Pwy oedd honna?' gofynnodd Arabela oedd yn sefyll o flaen Anna yn y rhes.

'O, hi, ym, wel, ym, Siriol Swyn,' meddai Anna gan faglu dros ei geiriau. 'Mae hi'n anobeithiol am greu swyn ac felly fe wnes i, ym, roi ychydig o, ym, gyngor munud olaf iddi hi ar gyfer y gystadleuaeth.'

'Wel, ti ydi swynwraig orau'r ysgol,' meddai Arabela'n llon.

Roedd Anna'n teimlo'n ofnadwy.

Doedd hi ddim yn hoffi dweud celwydd wrth ei ffrind gorau, ond doedd hi ddim eisiau ei siomi chwaith.

* * *

O'r diwedd, roedd yn bryd dechrau'r Prawf Swyn Blynyddol. Safai pob tylwythen deg o Ysgol y Naw Dymuniad yn eu grwpiau perthnasol, gan aros yn eiddgar a nerfus i'w henwau gael eu galw.

Bob yn un, daeth pawb i sefyll ar y llwyfan o flaen y Frenhines a Miss Pŵer, gan berfformio'r swyn gorau o fewn eu gallu. Roedd y tylwyth teg i gyd yn rhoi o'u gorau.

Fe fyddai'r marc roedden nhw'n ei dderbyn nid yn unig yn penderfynu ym mha ddosbarth y bydden nhw y flwyddyn nesaf, ond fe fyddai hefyd yn cyfrannu at benderfynu pa fath o dylwythen deg fydden nhw ar ôl

gadael yr ysgol. Roedd y mwyafrif o'r
tylwyth teg yn gwybod eisoes beth
hoffen nhw fod, ac felly'n gwneud eu
gorau glas i greu argraff ar eu
hathrawon.

'Siriol Swyn,' galwodd y Frenhines,
gan ddilyn trefn ei rhestr.

'Pob lwc!' galwodd Moli, Poli a Mali
wrth i Siriol gerdded ar y llwyfan.
Crynai adenydd Siriol wrth iddi
geisio canolbwyntio ac anghofio am

Anna am foment. Anadlodd yn ddwfn ac yna troelli'r ffon yn ysgafn ac yn uchel uwch ei phen, gan ganolbwyntio'n galed ar ei swyn.

Roedd swyn Siriol yr un mor berffaith ag yr oedd neithiwr yng Nghoed y Naw Dymuniad.

'Hyfryd!' meddai'r Frenhines, gan guro'i dwylo'n frwdfrydig. 'Siriol, fe ddylet ti fod yn falch iawn ohonot ti dy hun. Fe fyddi di'n sicr yn symud i ddosbarth uwch!'

Gwenodd Siriol o glust i glust a sgipio oddi ar y llwyfan i ymuno â'i ffrindiau.

'Roeddet ti'n wych!' meddai Poli a Mali gyda'i gilydd.

'Mae'n rhaid dy fod ti wedi treulio oriau'n ymarfer ar y funud olaf,' meddai Moli. 'Rwyt ti wedi trawsnewid o fod yn wirioneddol warthus i fod yn wirioneddol wych!'

Edrychodd Siriol o'i hamgylch ar bigau'r drain, yn chwilio am Anna.

Roedd yn falch ei bod
hi wedi gwneud
cystal yn y prawf,
ond roedd hi'n
poeni mwy am
sut roedd Anna
wedi perfformio.
Suddodd calon Siriol

wrth weld Anna ddagreuol yn
cofleidio Arabela. Roedd hi'n siŵr
y byddai ei chynllun wedi gweithio,
ond efallai ei bod hi'n anghywir.

'Mae'n ddrwg gen i,' meddai Siriol.

'Am beth?' holodd Arabela. 'Does
dim angen i ti deimlo'n flin dros
Anna – hi ydi seren y sioe!'

'Ond ro'n i'n meddwl dy fod ti'n
ddigalon?' meddai Siriol wedi drysu.

'Na, dwi wedi cael fy synnu a
mhlesio gyda chanmoliaeth
Brenhines y Tylwyth Teg, dyna'r
cwbl. Mae hi wedi fy nghodi i ddau
ddosbarth yn uwch.'

'Roedd Anna'n anhygoel,' meddai

Arabela'n falch. 'A dweud y gwir, dwi erioed wedi'i gweld hi'n perfformio swyn cystal â hynna o'r blaen. Dwi'n meddwl bod gen i dipyn o waith dal i fyny â hi!' ychwanegodd gan chwerthin.

Pwysodd Anna ymlaen ychydig a sibrwd yng nghlust Siriol. 'Diolch am nôl y llwch hud. Fe gest ti hwyl dda arni – dydi'r llwch erioed wedi teimlo mor bwerus!'

'Ti dy hun oedd yn gyfrifol am dy dalent di heddiw, a dim byd arall – dim hyd yn oed y llwch hud!' sibrydodd Siriol yn ôl.

Crychodd Anna ei thalcen yn ddryslyd.

'Mae gen i gyfrinach i'w rhannu gyda tithau hefyd,' aeth Siriol yn ei blaen gan anghofio sibrwd. 'Fues i ddim yng Nghoed y Naw Dymuniad amser cinio!'

'Fuest ti ddim yng Nghoed y Naw Dymuniad?' meddai Arabela, ar ôl

iddi glywed ail hanner y sgwrs.
'Pa fath o gyfrinach ydi hynny?'

'Un sy'n dangos cred, anogaeth, hyder a llwyddiant!' meddai Siriol gan gydio'n dynn yn Anna.

Y gyfrinach fwyaf un ar gyfer
gwireddu dy freuddwyd

ydi credu
ynot ti dy hun

EmmaThomson

Siriol Swyn

Ffwdan Ffasiwn
a storïau eraill

EmmaThomson

Siriol Swyn

Dymuno Dawnsio
a storïau eraill

EmmaThomson

Siriol Swyn

Ffrindiau am Byth
a storïau eraill

EmmaThomson

Siriol Swyn

Cwsg Cythryblus
a storïau eraill

Emma Thomson

Siriol Swyn

Gwyliau Gwych
a storïau eraill

Emma Thomson

Siriol Swyn

Paradwys Pinc
a storïau eraill

Emma Thomson

Siriol Swyn

Hwyl Hud
a storïau eraill

Emma Thomson

Siriol Swyn

Merlod Medrus
a storïau eraill

Emma Thomson

Siriol Swyn

Penbleth mewn Parti
a storïau eraill

Dewch i gwrdd â Siriol Swyn   tylwythen arbennig iawn!

Mae bywyd yn llawn antur i Siriol Swyn a'i ffrindiau ffyddlon!

Cyfrinachau Cyfareddol – Mae tylwythen deg newydd o'r enw Ela wedi dechrau yn Ysgol y Naw Dymuniad, ac mae Siriol – sydd bob amser yn gyfeillgar – yn dod yn ffrind da iawn iddi. Ond beth yw'r gyfrinach fawr sy'n rhaid iddi ei chadw?

Sialens y Siocled – Mae'r ffrindiau wedi penderfynu rhoi'r gorau i fwyta siocled am fis cyfan. Ond haws dweud na gwneud lle mae Siriol yn y cwestiwn! A fydd ei ffrindiau'n darganfod ei chyfrinach fawr?

Gweld y Gwir – Mae diwrnod y Prawf Swyn Blynyddol ar y gorwel, ac mae Siriol yn poeni na fydd yn llwyddo. Ond tybed a fydd Anna'n gallu ei helpu?

ISBN 978-1-84851-133-0

G

£3.99   www.gomer.co.uk

9 781848 511330

HOPE FOR HANNAH

Hannah French has always wanted more from life than her sleepy Dartmoor village can offer. On the wild moors, she loses herself in poetry and dreams of escape. Two brothers are eager to help: gentle, kind and sensitive William, a painter who yearns for a creative life in France or Italy; and rugged, dangerous and extravagant Ralph, who is equally keen to show Hannah the world outside Dartmoor — but at what cost? When events in Hannah's life take a devastating turn, she is no longer certain who she can trust . . .

Books by Linda Mitchelmore
in the Linford Romance Library:

GRAND DESIGNS